AF265126

RELEASE THE DEBT

Inspirational Testaments of Strength and Purpose

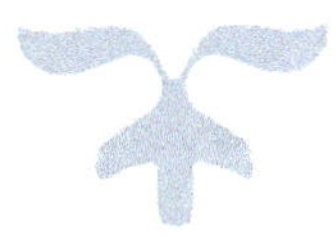

**Release the Debt
Inspiration Testaments of Strength & Purpose**

Copyright © 2018 by Bonita Parker Enterprises
All rights reserved.

This book or any portion thereof may not be reproduced, distributed or used in any manner whatsoever, including graphics, photography, or information storage without the express written permission of the publisher except for the use of reprints in the context of brief quotations, references, or book reviews.

Unless otherwise indicated, scripture quotations are from the Holy Bible, King James Version. All rights reserved.

Printed in the United States of America

ISBN 978-0-692-19170-5

Special discounts are available on bulk quantity purchases by book clubs and associations. For details, email:
bparker@bparkerenterprises.com

RELEASE THE DEBT

Inspirational Testaments of Strength and Purpose

DEDICATION

This book is dedicated to …

I know what you're thinking …

She wrote another book and did not even dedicate it to me.

Well guess what? You're wrong, *this book is for you.*

For all the teen girls who need a positive role model who has been through what they are currently going through. For the young adult women who are struggling to find their way and need guidance. And for the grown women who need encouragement and inspiration that they can overcome any obstacle and live the life of their dreams.

Forever and always,

Your Sister in the Journey

Bonita Parker

LIFE COACH & TRANSFORMATION STRATEGIST

TABLE OF CONTENTS

FOREWORD

Too often we allow actions of our past to overpower the person we are destined to become in a way that disables our ability to move forward in achieving our goals ...

Since I launched Nikki Woods Media several years ago, it has evolved a few times and *so have I.*

I have gone from being the producer of the nationally syndicated Tom Joyner Morning Show to embracing social media, gaining a massive audience and establishing a global presence, to becoming a bestselling author, to consulting with authors and other entrepreneurs on how to get the kind of media attention that will promote their brands and sell their products. I'm always interested in learning from other women and sharing ways to become more successful.

When Bonita reached out to me to write the Foreword for this book, I felt honored to be asked and very willing to urge others to read empowering stories by and about women. Not personally knowing her but becoming familiar with her work and the intent of this project, I agreed to write this piece because I am personally familiar with many of the issues discussed in her extremely relatable book. You can have many ideas, opportunities and businesses but some of us struggle with personal demons that are holding us back.

With many of my colleagues and clients being women, most of us have had to re-invent ourselves at least once personally and professionally.

Aside from my business endeavors, I am also the single mom of two teen-aged boys and have experienced the ups and downs of salary changes as I went from working for someone else to stepping out on faith and depending only on the income generated from my business, so Bonita's book definitely speaks to me and women like me.

This riveting anthology is of eight women who, through undying determination and unwavering faith, beat the odds to change their life. Release the Debt features inspirational stories from life coach and transformation strategist, Bonita Parker who brings together women who share their real-life experiences of how they broke free from the pain of consequential choices, fear-based decisions and emotional baggage in order to shift their narrative and not allow their challenges to hold them hostage.

The lessons imparted on these pages are designed to encourage you to push through the obstacles with astounding faith. These stories were written for you to understand that despite the challenges you face, there are lessons that you must grow through to get to the absolute best side of your life.

Bonita pulls out all the stops in this book! Her coaching work is highly visible in the writing of each author's story as she pushed them dig deep to uncover those invisible enemies that they buried deep down inside and encouraged them to provide step-by-step actions that helped them release and transition out of their internal debt.

Very inspiring read! ~ Nikki Woods

INTRODUCTION

When one hears the term "debt-free", they tend to think of being in a state of financial well-being. Most may think of paying off mortgages, car notes, credit cards and student loans. But what about the invisible debts … the heartaches, the pains, the warped mentality, disappointments and toxic behaviors that are left to fester and go unhanded … *unpaid*. What about those debts? The broken promises we make to ourselves, the feelings left unaddressed, the stuff that we constantly make excuses for that builds up in our core and affects the way we act and reflect within us by the decisions we make in life. I'm talking about *that* kind of debt … those invisible enemies that are hidden inside of us but still very much alive. The father who was never present in our lives, which left us looking for his love in other men. The mother who was so judgmental that we felt compelled to prove that we could measure up. The first boyfriend who cheated and left us feeling insecure about who we were.

What about these debts?

Because you see, I'm a firm believer that the way we are in our current life is a reflection of the hand that life has passed on to us. Those of us who shift the trajectory and change the narrative of our story are the ones that got a hold of the lesson early on … and those who are still in struggle … *well, they are still in class.*

So, when do you take these derogatory notations off the *credit report*? At what point do you say I've had enough … I'm tired of hurting … I'm sick of making costly decisions and mistakes that are costing me my best life?

Sadly enough, most can't begin to pinpoint when their emotional debt began because they've spent a great portion of their time masking old debt and piling on new debt. Have you ever heard the term, *"hurt people hurt people"*? When you are stuck in your emotional debt, you possess a very powerful negative energy or toxicity that is constantly seeking a way to release itself. It latches on to anything that could give it a recharge or boost, and in this state, it becomes easy for you to lash out or inflict unjust pain on others – especially those who had no connection to your pain whatsoever. And instead of releasing this pain you are carrying around, you make things worse by inflicting pain on others, or yourself, be it physically, emotionally or verbally.

My emotional debt began when my mother abandoned me. I spent a good portion of my adolescent life wondering if, and when, she would return, but she never did. What I didn't realize was that I had this wall of concrete built around my heart to disallow anyone from getting in and from me getting hurt or abandoned ever again. My motto in life was to leave them before they left me … to hurt them before they hurt me – and for many years *this worked.* I felt no pain nor remorse ... just protection. *So I thought ...*

In hindsight, this behavior will do more harm to your mental psyche than good. You may notice a hit to your self-esteem. Your confidence level may take a nose-dive (if it was ever there to begin with). As a result, you tend to make more and more excuses for your actions and decisions. *The mind plays tricks on you ...*

So how do you begin cleaning off your *credit report?*

After securing a life coach and through personal development work, I began to see a shift in the life I was living. Costly mistakes that I was making became more thought out and predetermined. I saw a major increase in my self-love and self-esteem. I was repaying debt and slowly but surely developing the mental tools for getting back to *me* and being a positive force in my circle.

I want to give you some of my very own strategies for breaking down the emotional barriers and living a debt-free life.

The first and most important step is *accountability.* Take ownership of your truth instead of trying to hide it or cover it up. When we learn to face our wrongdoings, it provides a freedom within us that allows for clarity and growth to take place. A shift in the narrative automatically takes place, your shoulders will suddenly relax, and things will look a lot differently for you.

The next strategy is to be more in tuned. More *aware*. Be the gatekeeper of your mind. Once the truth has prevailed, your level of being accountable for your own actions and decisions will increase. But this will involve you being really cognizant of those invisible enemies that have held you back previously. If you notice or feel yourself slipping into old thought patterns and decisions, it does not mean that you must go that route. Simply regroup and do the opposite.

Third, take actionable *risks*. Sometimes when we inject certain actions into our life to prevent another action from happening, we tend to forget that it started as a defense mechanism. We can't see the growth if we don't remove that mechanism – that hinderance. For example, when I was abandoned by my mother, I put up a wall and developed this pattern of leaving situations where I could potentially get hurt. To conquer that emotional barrier, I did the opposite and made the conscious decision to deal with whatever the outcome may turn out to be. If I got hurt in the end, I would accept it and deal with it so that I could grow from it. Sometimes growth involves taking risks and doing the things we wouldn't have otherwise done.

If you feel the weight of the invisible enemies – those emotional debts from your past that you've been holding on to, be honest about them and put awareness to the situation. And in no time, you will see a positive shift in your life unlike one you've never imagined.

And herein lies the concept of *"releasing the debt."*

ABOUT THE VISIONARY

 **BONITA PARKER** is a highly sought-after life and business transformation coach, 2x best-selling author and national speaker. She uses her voice to impact women using her transparent approach to being super radical to achieve your super possible best life.

Women are moved by her bold yet endearing message of walking authentically in your purpose and owning your mess. She trains audiences on how to overcome limiting beliefs and use fear as a positive tool to taking bold action to achieve their goals. She tells a highly impactful and inspirational story of conquering Stage 4 metastatic breast cancer in under eight months by developing a radical success mindset and making the decision to live her best life without fear and inhibitions.

Bonita is the CEO of *Bonita Parker Enterprises, LLC* and visionary of the *Unmask Yourself Symposium* and *Radical SuccessCon* life-changing conferences. In early 2018, she opened the virtual doors of the *Dream Achieve Win! Academy,* which houses her signature Radical Success business and personal development coaching programs for entrepreneurs and aspiring life coaches. She has been featured on the Dr. Oz show, in SHEEN Magazine, cocoaFAB Magazine and multiple other local media outlets.

True to her servant-heart and knack for giving back, Bonita founded the *WJP Foundation for Autism* where she advocates for children and families living with autism to pay tribute to her son who was assessed in 2014 and donates her time by speaking to and encouraging women who are battling breast cancer globally.

She currently resides in Waldorf, MD with her fiancé and 11-year old son.

Learn more about this author at: www.bonitaparker.com

LIFE AFTER DEBT

Written by

Dr. Vonetta C. Allen

Imagine waking up one morning and realizing your combined debt totaled $100k. Yeah, I know, that's kind of hard to imagine; right? Now try to imagine waking up one morning just a few years later completely debt free after bearing the burden from this magnitude of debt. Imagine having a lifelong history of struggling with your finances. You know the old adage… "Robbing Peter to Pay Paul". I somehow managed to master this art wreaking havoc over my personal finances. What I found interesting about my situation was no one knew or could even tell I was in such financial disarray. You see, on the outside looking in, I appeared to have it all together. After all, it was common practice to upgrade my vehicle every couple of years. In fact, there were a couple of times in which I traded in a vehicle within one year of ownership and a couple of times in which I owned two vehicles at the same time. To put things into perspective, I have now owned a total of 16 vehicles and three motorcycles in my lifetime. In hindsight, that was pretty reckless behavior to say the least. You're probably starting to see the audacious trend of how most of my financial troubles started.

One would probably think that I should have learned a lesson or two from my irresponsible, erratic spending behavior; however, that wasn't the case. You see, I also had a thing with credit cards. The constant use or should I say overuse and abuse of those evil credit cards is where the real problems began. I can't speak for anyone else, but I know I had a false sense of unlimited access to spending. Although there is clearly an established credit limit, I often felt the sky is the limit when using my credit cards. But, my limitless thought process and behavior eventually got me in big trouble or should I say mounds of debt as I continued to use my credit cards to buy whatever my heart desired. The sad thing is that I had several credit cards in my possession to choose from. As the transactions started stacking up and the cards came near the limit, I'd simply switch to the next. As long as I was making the minimum payment, I was good to go. Well, so I thought. Even though I was making the minimum payment on time, I noticed something strange was happening to my credit score. My credit score was dropping drastically and quickly! But, how could this be? No one warned me; no one told me about the negative impact a maxed-out credit card could potentially have on my credit report. I know at least my parents never taught me to be fiscally responsible. In fact, watching my parents when I was growing up and their relationship with money, I believed money was of scarcity and didn't know what a credit card was. I for certain knew and understood very well that "money did not grow on trees". Well as it would turn out, my credit score became the least of my worries. I had become so swipe-happy that eventually I ran out of cards to juggle. I ended up creating a payday loan situation with my credit cards. You know one of those temporary loans you get that must be paid back in part or in full on your next payday. Well at least it certainly felt like payday loan because I was using the bulk of my pay check just to pay the minimum payment on my credit cards, which created the need to use my credit cards to cover my daily living expenses such as food and fuel. I can tell you from experience, this is no way to live. Yet and still I put up such a facade that no one knew I was silently struggling to dig myself from the financial grave I dug for myself.

By now you're probably thinking, *why didn't you just put the credit cards away and stop using them.* I think it's fair to say that although it's logical to think that way, often times it's easier said than done. You see, there was a bigger underlying issue I had struggled with for many years. Quite honestly, I didn't even realize I had problems that were so deeply rooted until years later. In fact, it wasn't until after I kicked my "drug" habit that I learned my money problems were directly tied to my emotions and my mental state. Not those type of drugs silly rabbit... I'm talking the therapeutic type. You know the type that makes you feel good for the moment. I was literally self-medicating with "retail therapy." Unknowingly, I allowed myself to exist in a world of self-pity from different life experiences I endured over time. Its funny how life throws you curveballs and you're expected to automatically know how to deal with them, right? Well for me, I went through most of my life feeling incomplete. Most of the emotional instability I experienced was attributed to certain relationships and some hurt and pain caused by people in my life that I loved and trusted.

You see feeling unloved and unwanted as a child caused me to seek love and attention from all the wrong places when I was a teen. I ultimately fell in love with my high school sweetheart at the tender age of fifteen. This teenage love coupled with many more broken bonds and relationships would prove to be the start of many years of toting emotional baggage. I had to make many life changing decisions at an early age. In fact, while on my second pregnancy in high school I made the decision to obtain a GED or what some affectionately call the Good Enough Degree. At least it was good enough for me. It got me where I needed without much judgement, irony, or scrutiny. To be honest, most people that know me don't even know I have a GED and it's not something that I'm ashamed of at this point. This was a sound-minded choice that I made for me. I still remember quite vividly the day I approached the high school counselor with my bright idea to test out of school. I explained to her my situation with having a child at home and one on the way. The counselor was very understanding and suggested that I take a few classes to prep for the test. Although I appreciated her willingness and candid desire to help, I simply said, "ma'am I could just continue in my current classes and complete the credits to earn my high school diploma if that were the case. Can't I just take the test first to see how well I score, then take the enrichment classes for whichever subjects I may need additional help with? She agreed this was a good idea. I took the entire four-part test in one day and passed every subject area. This ended my high school nightmares and propelled me straight into the nightmares of the workforce. You know that thing that we all must do to earn a decent, honest living to take care of ourselves. Whoever said growing up was easy... I recognized early on that I would eventually need some additional education under my belt to at least be competitive in the workforce. But at this particular time, that was not at the top of my list of priorities.

Two short years after receiving my GED, I gave birth to my third child just four months shy of my nineteenth birthday. I was in an extremely toxic, abusive relationship until I mustard up the courage to walk away on my 21st birthday after having my lip split wide open in front of my kids. The funny thing though is that it wasn't the blow to my mouth that hurt as much as the words that came from his mouth when I left. "I hope you fail," he said. Oddly enough those words became a reminder of words I heard when I was a child. "you're sorry"," you're lazy," you will never amount to anything", and my favorite "you'll never keep a job. Imagine where I would be if I allowed any of those words to stunt my growth or stop me from working hard to get to where I am today. Now let me be clear, those words didn't stop me, but they were very damaging because I often found myself over the years reflecting on those words. I learned how damaging words can be and I live by the cliché. If you don't have anything nice to say, say nothing at all. Needless to say, I went through several years of feeling lonely, unloved, unwanted, and full of self-doubt. I literally felt like I was damaged goods. The sad thing is I didn't even know I was damaged. Many years later after I had gotten out of debt, I learned my financial problems were a direct result of my emotional and mental instability as well as the stress and depression I had collected over the years.

Upon learning my triggers and what caused me to get into debt, I realized rather quickly I had to get this debt under control. My main concern was the effect the debt would have on my credit. It would have probably been easy to file bankrupt and just forget all about the debt I had racked up, but the one thing that was stopping me from taking the easy way out was my financial management career field in the U.S. Air Force. My career field required me to have a security clearance. My credit history and how well I am with my finances is part of the process involved with being granted a security clearance. In my mind, my job was tied to my credit. Bad credit equals no security clearance which ultimately equals unemployment. Therefore, I knew my only option was to tackle the debt head on. One day I sat and made a list of all my debt to include my car note. I listed the type of debt, the amount of the debt, the amount of the payment, and the interest rate. I started knocking out the debt with the smallest balance and the largest interest rate first. I made a budget and I stuck with it. I used any excess cash to throw larger payments on a single card until it was paid off. Those small wins equated to bigger wins once they were all paid off. Now, I don't want to be misleading in any way because it wasn't as easy as I make it sound and what you need to know is that aside from my military employment, I ended up working multiple jobs to secure additional income for my mission to pay off debt… #OperationDebtPayoff. And who said, you can't have life after debt?

In the fall 2005, I took an H&R Block income tax course. The income tax course was a $300 investment, but in the end, it was well worth the investment. Although I was already doing taxes for friends and family, I had to take the three-month class as a condition of employment regardless of my educational background or prior income tax preparation experience. I began working at H&R Block in January 2006 and I loved working for the tax preparation giants in the income tax industry. Working at H&R Block kept me busy preventing me from spending extra money and it allowed me to earn the extra money I needed to pay towards my debt. At the end of the first tax season working for the company, my final check contained an end of season bonus, which basically was the remaining commission left from my weekly pay draws. In my first year working for H&R Block, I was only expecting a few hundred dollars in my commission bonus check. I thought my weekly pay draws had consumed the bulk of the commission I earned; however, to my surprise, I had earned a bonus of $2,500 in just three short months of part time work. I was excited to say the least. Not only was I excited, I was both grateful and motivated. I was grateful because the bonus allowed me to chip away at some of the debt that I felt crippled and stifled my growth for so long. I was motivated and couldn't wait to return the next tax season anticipating another big win. Now, you may not think $2,500 is much; however, for someone struggling with debt, that $2,500 was a lot! The next year rolled around and I could hardly wait to get inside H&R block's doors and start doing what I really enjoyed; taxes! You see working at H&R block felt more like a hobby to me rather than a job because I was doing something I actually loved doing. I was good at it, and I was making good money doing it. Working at H&R Block was a win, win situation in my book. At the start of the tax season, I learned my hourly rate had increased mainly because I had such a high bonus at the end of the previous tax season. My initial thought was welp it looks like my bonus won't be as much this year since I'm getting paid more up front. Oh well it'll alright, I thought. The end of the tax season came quick, which typically happens when you're enjoying what you do. As they say, time flies when you're having fun. I was excited to see what my bonus would look like; however, I had to wait patiently for the final compensation to be calculated before I would receive my bonus. It was usually a two-week period, but I waited patiently as I did the year prior. I will tell you I was shocked and amazed when the bonus check finally came out along with the compensation report. I earned approximately $5,000 in commission bonus in my second year. That's right, I freaking doubled my bonus from the year prior. Oh, you couldn't tell me a thing! I was on fire! I was doing the damn thing! I realized quickly that returning clients was the key to being successful at H&R Block and I strived to ensure I provided excellent customer service and did a phenomenal job preparing income taxes. By the end of my third tax season with H&R Block and the seasons to come, I was earning a whopping $7,500 plus in commission bonus. I later went on to start my own income tax business in 2009 at the advice of others and taking that leap of faith. My entrepreneurial success doesn't start nor stop here.

At the end of the first tax season at H&R Block as I patiently awaited the start of the next tax season in anticipation of my next win, I couldn't help but think, "what now"? What can I do now to earn additional income until the start of the next tax season? I recall thinking back on how intrigued I've always been with the success my father had with real estate. My father had an entrepreneurial spirit and owned a couple of businesses during his time. He also owned seven properties free and clear of a mortgage before he passed away in August 1991, just a few short days before my 17th birthday. Most of the homes my father owned were purchased in the 70s, which was a major accomplishment for an African American male during those oppressed times to say the least. In fact, I became intrigued with the idea of real estate and the thought of real estate investing resonated with me the more I thought about my father and his endeavors. That's it, I thought. I'll take a real estate course. By the end of June 2006 shortly after the tax season had ended, I was enrolled in a real estate course. The interesting fact about that is I never set out to obtain a real estate license. I was only taking the course to learn about real estate so I can get into investing. The instructor convinced me that obtaining my real estate license is the way to go even if my plans are to invest in real estate vs practicing real estate. Either way, I'm happy I took his advice. I went on to take the state test and became licensed in September 2006. I had my first real estate settlement in December 2006 and went on to close another seven transactions in my first year by August 2007. All while working a full-time job serving my country and oh by the way did I mention I was working on earning my Master of Business Administration degree which I completed in December 2008. Shortly after earning my MBA, I began teaching at Columbia College. All the while, I continued to knock down my debt with the extra income I was earning until they were all gone.

Now while I don't advise anyone to go as hard as I did, I would say figure out what gift or your niche is and start there. Make sure it's something you absolutely enjoy doing. In the end it will feel rewarding, effortless, and you will have that burning desire to stick to it. On the other hand, if you don't enjoy what you're doing, it will feel much like work and you may end up resenting what you're doing which will show up in the quality of your craftsmanship. You never want that to happen because depending on what your line of business is, it could potentially be detrimental to the success of your business.

If you find yourself in a similar situation where you are spending out of control and you wake up one day and realize you too are buried in a mound of debt, please know that you are not alone. I too have been there and there are many others just like you and I that are in the same situation or that may have been there and managed to find a way out. In fact, some of your closest friends or family members may be in that very situation but choose not to share just as I chose not to share when I was desperately struggling to keep my head above water. However, I am a living, breathing, walking, talking testimony that there is life after debt. You must find your own way and figure out what strategy works best for you and your own individual situation because no two situations are ever the same. What may work for me or someone else, may not work for you. No matter what direction you decide to go in to get back on track by all means be deliberate, be consistent, and stay focused. But whatever you do, never give up! Life happens, and you may just get knocked off your feet. However, if you hang in there and weather the storm, you will always find that calm after the storm. Below are a few tried and true tips that may prove to be helpful and propel you forward into living your best life after debt.

1. If you know you're overwhelmed, anxious, stressed, depressed, or dealing with any sort of ailment, please do yourself a favor and seek professional help. Do not be afraid or ashamed to seek help. Do not attempt to "self-medicate" as I once did and create additional strife in your life. Some of the things I've found to help deal with stress and depression is exercising in general, yoga, massages, acupuncture, and talking to someone I can trust. There are ways to benefit from each without breaking the bank especially if you're already in debt. You can always exercise in the comfort of your home at no cost or maybe even go out for a walk or a run. There are several YouTube videos out that you can follow to get into a good yoga workout routine. Utilize your significant other or a friend to give you that good massage you've been needing all day. It may not be as good as a professional massage session; however, the idea is to get some self-time and relax. Acupuncture treatments can be a bit pricy, but a good health insurance plan can make acupuncture affordable as you'll only be responsible for small payments based on the terms of your plan.

2. You don't know what you don't know… Educate yourself. Knowledge is power, and you will be amazed at how much different your life or your life's situations will change with each additional nugget of information you obtain. When you know better, you do better… Research it. Do your due diligence and research the information you don't know or the information you think you may need to know to get started. Google is your friend. Use it! If you don't know where to start with getting your finances on track, do some homework. There are tons of information on finances and getting out of debt. Phone a credible friend that may be in a position to help or at least point you in the right direction. We all have that one friend that is full of good advice. Leverage your resources.

3. When all else fails, pray about it! God still answers prayers. Be deliberate in your prayers. Ask God for exactly what it is you want and then get into action. As my father use to say, "The good Lord helps those whom helps themselves." If you're struggling financially and need a good prayer to help you get through some of those trying times, here's a simple prayer you can start with:

Lord, I am thankful for the financial resources with which You have blessed me. I want to be a good steward, a wise manager, of the resources You have entrusted to me. Help me to save and spend with discernment and to give to others in need. Help me to find balance – not be a hoarder

or an out-of-control spender. Give me a godly view of money and how to use it in ways that will honor You.
~ Jackie M. Johnson

ABOUT THE AUTHOR

DR. VONETTA C. ALLEN is a Financial Manager in the US Air Force, proudly serving for over 20 years. She is a licensed realtor, real estate investor, and mother to five beautiful children. She earned her Doctor of Business Administration from Walden University. Dr. Allen's goal is to leverage her educational and entrepreneurial journey to inspire women to channel their inner-selves and reach new heights of success through faith and perseverance.

RESILIENCE

Written By

Regina Clay

You are reading this and asking, *"How can I let it shine when I don't have enough money to pay my bills?"* ... *"How can I let it shine when the kids are just overwhelming me, and I am doing it all by myself?"* ... *"How can I let it shine when I receive no child support?"* ... *"How can I let it shine when I am in one of the darkest places in my life?"*

I say YOU CAN LET IT SHINE because it is YOUR TIME to SHINE. There was a time in my life when I asked these exact same questions, so I know what it feels like to be a single mom who is just barely holding on.

Single mothers come in a variety of types. According to the U.S. Census Bureau, there are about twelve million single parents. Today, one in four children under the age of 18—a total of about 17.4 million—are being raised without a father and nearly half (45%) live below the poverty line. Half have one child; 30% have two. 37.2% of custodial single mothers are 40 years old or older. These are statistics, but STATISTICS DON'T DEFINE OR LIMIT YOU.

Being a single mother is not always easy. I had my daughter at 39 and my son at 43 and became a single mom about a year after my son was born. Single Motherhood was not my destiny, so I thought but I also know that GOD told me that I deserved to be happy. I know a little something about marriages because I was married to both of my children's fathers. There is no history of divorce in my lineage. For example, my parents have been married over 50 years. My grandparents on both sides were married over 50 years. Yet, when I was not happy in my marriage, my mother insisted that I get out of it. For her to say, "Regina, it's not working. You've tried your best. File for divorce because I'm concerned that something really bad may happen." I knew that my situation must have been alarming. You see I had only been married 18 months to both my daughter and my son's fathers.

In hindsight, I now understand that I've always been seeking what my parents had or what I perceived they had. And that's why I always wanted a committed relationship that would lead to marriage. Only after two failed marriages and two children later, did I discover the REAL ME. I learned why I sought getting married so quickly rather than first being healthy and whole by MYSELF before committing to marriage. I wanted the "idea" of marriage because I thought it was what I was supposed to do—but not the "work" of marriage.

Iyanla Vanzant says, "When we lose a loved one to death or end a long-term relationship, it is perfectly normal to grieve. We must honor and recognize each stage of the grief and every emotion we have. When we do not grieve, we get stuck. We owe it to ourselves and the memory of the relationship to grieve and cleanse our soul."

I remember one day after my divorce watching my mom and dad plan a trip together. As I sat in the family room, I heard them interact. I stared out the window thinking, "I want what my parents have." Tears started rolling down my face as I began questioning myself, "Why don't I have a loving marriage? Why can't I get this right? What's wrong with me?" I was so caught up in my own world of thoughts that I didn't realize that my mom was standing next to me. I tried to hide my tears, but I couldn't fool her. She said, "Regina, you are a powerful young lady. You are NOT defined by any situation. Your life is your life." Our eyes locked and I felt incredibly at peace. I said, "Thank you Mom. I love you." "I love you too." We hugged.

My daughter is currently in 10th grade and my son is in 6th grade. They are both exceptional students, outstanding athletes in their own sports and lovable children. My biggest struggle as a single Mom was finances!!! How to pay the bills? How do you expose your children to the greater things in life? As I said, both of my children play sports and that cost money. Many nights I cried and often I was very depressed. There were mornings I did not want to get out of bed. While my children are my greatest joy and most definitely are one of the main reasons I remain Resilient despite it all it is challenging to balance finances by yourself. Having joint custody with my son's father and lack of consistent child support the struggle was real. They watched me come home to a house of darkness because I had not paid the bill and the lights were off. They watched me cry many nights although I hid it from them most of the time.

Often single mothers must take on a second job because the ends are not meeting. Taking on another job causes mothers to be away from their children more often than they desire. I know because I have been there. I got involved in a Direct Selling Organization, so I could maximize my income and still have more time with my children.

I remember how miserable I felt when I had to buy a new car. I had not had a car payment in over four years, so the idea of monthly payments was scary. I walked into the dealership with my head hanging low. I wanted a nice car, but the payment had to be within my financial means. And to make matters worse, my credit was not the best. So, I just knew my payment would be high. Time passed slowly as I sat in the dealer's office waiting for him to do the numbers. He said, "Ms. Clay, I did the best I could." I sat on the edge of my seat terrified as to what he going to say next. Everything went into slow motion as I wanted to run out the door because of the embarrassment I would feel knowing the price was too high. I braced myself for the disappointment. And when he finally said what my monthly payment would be, I couldn't believe it. I leaped for joy. My Traci Lynn Jewelry business could pay that note! For the last five years, my car note has been low enough for me to keep my JOB—Just Over Broke—money in my pocket.

The CEO and founder of Traci Lynn Jewelry says, "The system works, and the system pays me," and this is so true.

My days are full—I run from sun up to sun down. Whether I am studying to deliver a speech, meditating on how to better serve my children, during a five-mile run, or helping meet the needs of a client, I am on the go. Time flies by so fast. But one lesson I've learned is that I must make time to empower myself spiritually, mentally, physically, and financially every day.

I have been empowered since I was a small child. My parents incredibly prepared me for my adult journey. They provided a great home life, a tremendous church life, and exposure to the realities of political life. Their multi-faceted exposure created the inner drive within me to make a positive difference with my life.

In life, we can sometimes be running so fast and so hard that we're not taking care of ourselves. And if we're not taking care of ourselves, we won't have anything to give to anyone else and that includes our children.

My Revelations:

1. I did not allow myself time to grieve my previous relationships because I was busy concentrating on the idea that I was a failure.

2. Given my competitive nature, I never want to fail. So rather than be alone, I would enter another relationship without really considering whether it was the best for me.

3. It is vital to be comfortable with yourself before you invite someone else into your space. You must be WHOLE and COMPLETE within yourself. To truly attract your soul mate, you must make sure <u>you</u> are whole first.

Through therapy, I was able to discover my true authentic self. I discovered my Why and my Purpose. Prior to getting some counseling, I was just drifting and operating in what I "thought" I was supposed to be doing in life. It is very easy to get stuck in a comfortable place, the easy place, the cruising place. But I had to move into the uncomfortable place to reach my destiny. Instead of staying docked at the bay and wearing a mask, I had to go out into the unknown to discover my truth.

"FEED YOUR FAITH and YOUR FEARS will STARVE TO DEATH." We must keep feeding our faith with positive things.

"FACE IT to FIX IT." If you don't face what the reality is, you will surely operate in fear.

Once I got out of fear, my destiny was awaiting right around the corner. However, when you are at your greatest moment of mastery, your past will pay you a visit—in many different forms.

Although I had mastered an addiction while in college, I still lived with the fear of failure. I often procrastinated, thinking that if I never started a project or never pursued my destiny, I would never fail because I never tried. Sometimes, life will have to "wake you up" so you get serious about your life. It certainly happened to me.

One evening, after dropping my daughter off for a sleepover, I went home to have a relaxing moment. I had a couple glasses of wine and was enjoying my alone time when my daughter called to say that she did not want to stay at the sleepover. Immediately I jumped into the car and started driving. Soon there were lights flashing behind me. After I pulled over, the officer asked, "Have you been drinking, Ms. Clay?" My daughter was scared and called my mother who lived a mile away and my mother came and intervened. The police still gave me citations and I went to court to face my consequences which included probation and multiple fines. I decided it was time to get help from someone outside of myself. I had been trying to do it alone for so long.

This was a defining moment for me. Up until that point, I just existed, going through the motions. At this point is when I decided to go to a therapist. Of course, in the community which I am from "we" don't seek therapy because that means you are crazy. I put all that aside and sought the help I needed. THERAPY is NOT the ENEMY. Through therapy, I was able to discover my true authentic self. I discovered my Why and my Purpose. Prior to getting some counseling, I was just drifting and operating in what I "thought" I was supposed to be doing in life. It is very easy to get stuck in a comfortable place, the easy place, the cruising place. But I had to move into the uncomfortable place to reach my destiny. Instead of staying docked at the bay and wearing a mask, I had to go out into the unknown waters to discover my truth.

Without even really knowing, I was sinking deeper and deeper into a sunken place. If I continued along this journey, I could see myself on medication for depression, sick with major illness, or who knows what else. But, with all the emotional and physical strength I could muster, I began to pull myself out of the gloomy place because I knew my children needed me. You may be wondering how I begin and I will tell you the first step is to recognize that you need help and find some qualified people to help you. It was my children who were my saving grace. I had to do it for them. They are my "Why?"

Sometimes in life, we need a major wake-up call to get our attention prompting us to be more conscious as to how we are *really* living. For every choice we make, there is a consequence. Being pulled over by the police officer was my wake-up call to be better, to do better, to live better and to live my best life. I had to the RELEASE the DEBT of FEAR.

Have you already had your wake-up call? How did you change? How did you grow?

Today, I am more conscious and intentional about who I choose to spend my time with because it matters. I choose to spend my time with uplifting and encouraging people who truly want me to be my absolute best. And this has made all the difference in the world.

To breakthrough in your life, you must hook up with the right people. Sometimes one mentor might provide all your needs, but I needed a team approach. I have three mentors who mentor me on different levels: Dr. Frank M. Reid III, my spiritual mentor; Dr. Traci Lynn, my entrepreneur mentor; and Delatorro McNeal, my speaking mentor.

Make sure the right people push you, drive you, fuss at you, and love on you all at the same time. Who are the five closest people in your life right now whose advice and opinion you accept the most? Now answer this profound question: Do each of these five people really want what's best for you?

Be courageous and make the necessary changes because this is your life.

Have you ever been through a storm, hurricane, or snowstorm where your whole house loses power? Have you ever had a moment of complete darkness in your life? Life will take on new meaning. It's your time to shine!

Dr. Martin Luther King said, "Faith is taking the first step even when you can't see the entire staircase."

Often, we think we are alright where we are but often we need a life challenge to slap us in the face to give us the wake-up call that is needed to propel us to the next dimension. If I could offer you anything through reading my story to help you release the baggage within you it would be the following:

1. Remove the Obstacles: You know what these obstacles are and if you don't find yourself a coach, mentor or friend you trust to help you. Obstacles are opportunities for growth. I would not be where I was without the obstacles including divorce, DUI and FEAR.

2. Connect with the right people. Evaluate your circle. Are they always speaking negative and doom and gloom? Change your circle

3. Connect with a POWER SOURCE. You must get connected with something greater than yourself. Whatever it is, it must be greater than you and what you can imagine. If it is not than it is not the right source.

Take the first step TODAY because it's your time to shine!

This little light of mine I'm going to let it shine.
This little light of mine I'm going to let it shine.
This little light of mine I'm going to let it shine.
Let it shine, let it shine, let it shine!!

ABOUT THE AUTHOR

 **REGINA CLAY** has a special gift of connecting with persons from across the country in various industries. She received her B.A. degree in Communications from the University of Virginia and her Master of Divinity degree from Howard University School of Divinity. Regina is an ordained minister and uses that gift to speak and teach globally.

Having been a single mother herself, Regina places women's organizations who advocate for single mothers at the core of her service. She also specializes in political consulting and developing faith-based and non-profit organizations. Throughout her life and through every obstacle, Regina has possessed the fortitude to transform her life and she teaches others how to do the same through her transparent story.

Learn more about this author at www.reginaclay.com

NO MORE WOE IS ME

Written by

Anita Galloway

It was happening again. Raging violence and disrespect at the hands of the man who said he would always love and protect me. I had little time to ready myself for the one-sided fight that would again leave me bloodied and bruised. How in the world had I landed myself back in this same situation; cowering in fear before a man whose only intent seemed to be complete destruction of my womanhood. I was tired of this familiar act of victimization and was suddenly overcome with an air of defiance. Gathering my courage, I told him that if he laid a finger on me again, I would have him arrested. As a black woman, I knew that calling the police on a black man was considered a cardinal sin by many in our community, but for once, I did not let that damper my resolve. It was him or me and I had finally had enough. He relented and left my house spewing hateful words that, at a different point in time, would have left me feeling like a victim, but instead I felt empowered. I had, in a sense, exorcised the demon of victimization and reclaimed my self-respect and power. Not all in one sitting of course, but I had taken that powerful first step. I decided on that day that I would no longer be held hostage by the ghosts of my past that manifested themselves in toxic romantic relationship. Free to explore my true self and reclaim my life, I reflected on my past and wondered; how did I become ensnared in the cycle of victimization? Why was I plagued by low self-esteem, neediness and emotional insecurity? What was it that happened in my past that made me a prime candidate for victimization in my future? It took years of therapy and practice in self-actualization to dredge up and release the debt of pain and trauma from my past that formed the patterns of dysfunction in my life. I no longer view myself as a victim but as a survivor and it is with this mindset that I approach life, secure in the knowledge that while there will be plenty of obstacles on my path, my past and its pain would not be one of them.

As I set out on my journey of healing through self-examination, reconciliation and release, I knew that as a survivor of child sexual abuse, I was prone to unhealthy and compulsive behavior in relationships, but what I didn't know was exactly how and why the abuse I sustained in childhood, reared its ugly head in romantic relationships and subjected me to violence and abuse as an adult, compelling me to hitch my life to people who were manipulative, unhinged and sometimes sadistic. My love life was a revolving door of pain and disappointment, costing me many sleepless nights and angst-ridden days. I approached relationships from a position of weakness; as if I had nothing of substance to offer believing that I was damaged goods, beyond the repair of hope, grace and mercy. My childhood victimization played on like a broken record in my life until I decided that it was time to finally assert myself as a survivor and not a victim. I knew that my prospects for a happy future would improve once I was armed with knowledge that gave a name to my reckless tendencies and behaviors.

Many counseling experts call it a silent killer: Revictimization is a detrimental, and oftentimes lifelong, byproduct of childhood abuse or interpersonal violence (domestic violence for example) that exposes survivors to additional trauma or abuse later in life. Very often, revictimization exist as the rule rather than the exception in survivors of abuse. In fact, many individuals who experience sexual or physical abuse have a very high chance of experiencing some other form of abuse in the future, be it mental, emotional or psychological. The pattern of revictimization can be woven by the victim developing anxiety, depression or post-traumatic stress disorder (PTSD) after they have been victimized. Abuse greatly alters the victims' decision-making abilities, clouds judgement and promotes compulsive behavior and traumatic bonding. Without therapy, self-help and healing, the revictimization cycle flourishes, but it is possible to break through the arrested development and build a life that is meaningful, secure and emotionally debt free-here is how I did it.

Very early in my childhood, I learned many things that would become the blueprint for how I operated in adulthood including the value of hard work, the importance of a strong work ethic and how to suffer in silence. Our family had a newspaper route delivering the *Washington Post,* we delivered close to three hundred papers every day for five years; it was grueling but productive work. I was eleven years old when one morning, my life's trajectory was changed forever. I became the victim of a serial rapist who later threatened to kill me if I revealed his identity. My unwillingness to identify my abuser sealed my fate as a voiceless victim and set in motion a pattern of promiscuity, violence and abuse. Out of fear, I let my abuser off the hook and he was free to continue his predatory ways, victimizing other young girls for another two years before he was finally caught and brought to justice. After his capture, I thought that everything associated with that assault was behind me, little did I know, I was signed up for a lifetime of repeatedly living the ordeal because as a victim whose trauma went unchecked, I was subconsciously replicating my victimization in the relationships I chose to pursue. This led to a personal life that was littered with deep disappointment, anxiety and self-inflicted pain.

What many people may not know, is that there is a clear-cut relationship between childhood sexual abuse and substance abuse later in life. Research shows, that early sexual victimization may promote substance abuse and consensual sexual behavior with multiple partners which increases the likelihood that victims will encounter potential perpetrators later in life.

By the time I was twenty-nine, I became involved in a romantic relationship with a heavy drinker whose violent mood swings raged on, undeterred by my pregnancy, my pleas for mercy or the presence of my children. I formed a traumatic bond with this man and to dull the pain of this abusive relationship, I turned to alcohol and drugs. Things between he and I started off smoothly enough. Because he was my childhood friend, we often spent time together sharing details about our relationships and different personal and social interactions. He knew about my childhood abuse and was always very compassionate and gentle when giving me advice on relationships and how to deal with men. I let him convince me that we would make excellent parents and that marriage was on the horizon. I was so tired of the fits and starts of the relationships and situationships that I was involved in, that I did not take the time to get to know this man as an adult. In typical victim fashion, I let him drive the relationship, determine my worth and make plans for my own future. My childhood sexual abuse and the feelings of betrayal that accompanied it led me to long for a re-established trust in others but my poor judgment about which individuals were trustworthy always stymied my efforts. This romantic relationship was no different. Also, as a child sexual abuse survivor, I suffered from anxious attachment which rendered me desperate, clingy and needy, not believing that I had any value to add to a relationship except sex. I was willing to hack off an arm in the name of love is this man asked me to. I was a mess. A great sense of powerlessness prevented me from asserting myself in this, and other relationships. Because this individual knew so much about me, including my risky and promiscuous sexual behavior, I was afraid he would stigmatize me and leave. In short, I endured unimaginable abuse at the hands of this man, right under the noses of my family and friends because my negative self-image would not allow me to out this monster nor would it allow me to believe I deserved better. It wasn't until he slapped me in the doctor's office while I was holding our newborn infant that I found the courage to leave. This was no moment of victory for me or great instance of self-actualization. People pleasing even in my darkest moments, I begged my abuser to seek help, to join me in therapy. I told him I forgave him for his violence and abuse. He told me that even if I were on fire he wouldn't piss on me. That I was a waste of space, someone who would never find love because no one wanted a slut for a wife and that he had wasted an orgasm on me because I was the dumbest, dirtiest, most unfit mother who ever walked the earth. Yet still, I begged him to stay. He refused, and I set about the business of dealing with the break up by nearly drinking myself to death.

My road to alcohol abuse was slow, winding and riddled with one dangerous encounter after another. One minute I was a social drinker and the next I was hitting the bottle every morning before work. I was a closet alcoholic. Only those in my inner circle knew how much I drank but even they didn't know the extent of my depravity. During my darkest days with alcohol, I blacked out so often I would wake up and not know where I was, I had scads of sexual encounters with people I wouldn't even recognize today. I was a mean, angry drunk with violent streaks I called ragers, a neglectful and impatient mother who had frequent brushes with Child Protective Services and almost lost my children and my teaching license. I tried to numb the sadness, resentment, pain and anger of my abuse with alcohol and random sex. Obviously, it didn't work. It only served to squeeze the life out of me and set me on an even greater path to destruction. Unfortunately, for survivors of child sexual abuse, those tasked with protecting and caring for them have no idea how transformative and harmful the abuse is, nor do they have a clue as to how far reaching the impact of not receiving therapy or counseling extend. It was too late for me at this point, or so I thought, but God had other plans.

My mother has always been a smart, hardworking woman who instilled in my sisters and me a solid work ethic, an independent spirit and a quick wit. My father was the strong silent type, full of gentle wisdom and compassion who taught me to never stop learning about the universe and the human spirit.   My parents' romantic relationship ended after my toddler stage. My father had always been present in my life, spending time with me and contributing to my financial well-being; but because he wasn't in the home with me, his presence in my life was not impactful enough for me to feel that I was growing up cherished, prized and protected. I did not have it easy growing when it came to the physicality's that the larger society praised and valued. I was teased and bullied for being dark-skinned, having been called hateful names like black and ugly, tar baby and black spot. I desperately needed the validation, approval and praise of who I was as a black girl growing up in a white, patriarchal society. I received those needful, soul sustaining things too late from my father. It wasn't until I was about sixteen years old that he changed the way he parented me and attempted to help me feel safe and secure, a feeling that I had yearned for as a little girl. The delayed response of my father's nurturing and my sexual assault had already set the blueprint for my romantic and sexual behavior.

From the time I was a teen, new to the dating game, until the time I was knocking on forty's door, I consistently developed strong emotional ties to people who intermittently harassed, beat, and threatened me. Along the trail of my trauma, I had confused pain with love and developed relationship attachments that constantly renewed the terror of abuse and abandonment. Because of my poor judgement and inability to overcome realistic fears, I longed for and attracted partners who were hyper aggressive, possessive and emotionally unavailable. Having been exposed to early abuse and feelings of abandonment, I was vulnerable to engaging in violent romantic relationships and because of my high arousal to stress in my toxic relationships, I continued to engage in the familiar pain of a traumatic bonding regardless of the rewards or repercussions.

I was so used to dysfunction and trauma in a relationship that I disassociated myself from my abuse. I preferred the familiar pattern of pain to the thought of exploring a loving alternative. One of my abusers had taken the level of abuse that I experienced by my previous abusers to another level altogether; causing injuries so severe that he literally rearranged my face. Even still, I stayed and in my dark, twisted mentality, I felt sorry for him! I wracked my brain and spent countless hours reading trying to uncover what ills he suffered in childhood that made him such a monster. I was determined to save him from himself and heal his heart. I continued to offer him my love, forgiving him unconditionally for the worst treatment and the most outrageous betrayals. I came to believe that he mattered more than me. It was my broken sense of self and the element of revictimization that kept me tethered to that hellish relationship. My violator was also my comforter but that did not matter because I longed for attachment and acceptance. His dual roles as both violator and comforter further cemented my sense of entrapment, which in my warped mind read as a happily ever after. Because I had an inaccurate assessment of danger, I was blamed for not being able to second-guess that this man would be a batterer. There was a tendency on my part to fall in with anyone who acted "nice", naively believing that they were nice, even when niceness was alternated with cruelty. On the part of family, friends and associates, I had to ward off insulting conclusions drawn about me and my intelligence. I was called everything from sick and sadistic to idiotic and stupid. Many people who victim blame do not understand that after layer upon layer of trauma has been piled on you, there is a tendency to have a skewed sense of reality and a lack of self-care that those who have not suffered childhood trauma cannot relate to. In my mind, child abuse can be likened to cancer, if left untreated the malignancy of the trauma can metastasize into protracted dangers that can eventually prove fatal.

Releasing the Debt ...

After the shock, numbness, denial, disbelief, resentment and anger of having been victimized and revictimized, I knew it was now time for the recovery. As an educator, I strongly believe that it is far easier to repair a damaged child than it is to repair a damaged adult. That said, the best line of defense when it comes to victimization and revictimization is prevention. Be as wary of family and friends around your children as you are of strangers. Explicitly teach them about staying on the safe side and having a keen sense of danger.

A second line of defense against revictimization is therapeutic counseling. Providing early intervention to abuse survivors is critical to helping them cope with their trauma so that they do not carry their damage into adulthood and live in a distorted reality anchored in their unchecked anguish. I did not have the benefit of early intervention therapy, so my teen, young adult and mid-adult years were mired in dysfunction and discord. Just as my path to misery and strife did not happen overnight, neither did my path to self-love, self-acceptance and self-respect.

My healing began when I entered rehab for my alcohol abuse. It was during this time that I came clean to my loved ones about my real problems and demons, I was so good at masking misery that my friends did not know the extent of my trauma and addictions. I began receiving individual and group therapy, finally being able to talk earnestly and honestly about my feelings and troubles was liberating. I began to allow myself to feel the pain of my life experiences and examined what stressors in my life triggered a replay of my past trauma. I have always been a bit of a loner and enjoyed spending time along, so during down times in rehab, I read different books on human behavior and development.

The book that by far has had the greatest impact on me is the standard issue brown book from Alcoholics Anonymous - *One Day at A Time*. It highlighted the importance of bringing God into my healing and waiting on him for daily guidance and direction.

I also learned the power of forgiveness, specifically forgiving myself. I did not realize how impatient and scornful I was with myself. Having been subjected to so much verbal, mental and emotional abuse, I came to believe that I was worthless. It was hard work changing that ever present narrative that was on repeat in my brain, but my support system was unyielding, and I began to put those old, useless thoughts to bed once and for all.

I learned to take care of both my mind and my body. Yoga, Pilates and walking became my constant companions, providing me with a release of tension, stress, doubts and fears. My family and my circle of friends, heading my hugh and cry, rallied around me and took great pains to ensure that I was safe and free of harm.

Releasing the debt of my past is an act that I practice earnestly each day. It has required a complete lifestyle change and has yielded incredible, healing results. I can now happily proclaim that I am debt free and that I have found my voice, my tribe and am in total possession of myself. I don't have all the answers but what I do have is a wonderful family, great group of friends and a future so bright I can scarcely contain my joy. On my journey of debt release I have learned many things but I leave you with this…

-just as there is a time of pain and sadness, there is a time for healing and recovery.

ABOUT THE AUTHOR

ANITA GALLOWAY is a career educator with more than a decade of classroom teaching experience. She has long believed that an investment in knowledge pays the best interest. To that end, she has worked to help others invest in their potential and achieve social, emotional and academic success.

A Washington, D.C. native and veteran teacher in the District of Columbia Public Schools system, Anita prides herself on creating communities of global learners through an unwavering commitment to the guiding principles and beliefs that reflect the values of an erudite society. A lifelong learner herself, Anita is a Japan Fulbright Scholar and a Yale National Initiative Fellow. She holds a B.A. in English/Secondary Education, an M.A. in Administration/Supervision and an M.A. in English as a Second Language. At the heart of Anita's educational philosophy is the belief that education is not preparation for life; education is life itself.

DETERMINED AGAINST ALL ODDS

Written by

Dana Hicks-Hungerford

Welcome to the world of Dana Hicks-Hungerford. Dana Hicks started out being an independent thinker at birth. I was raised in a two-parent household by very straightforward, hard-working and fun-loving parents. Being the oldest and the only girl with two younger brothers, I always felt like the leader. My parents taught us at a very young age to have your own mind. Some of the most valuable lessons taught by my parents were to always be unapologetically me and to never give up. They also taught me that in life there will be rules that you have to follow, but never lose yourself in the midst of the eyes of society. Both of my parents went to college and had awesome careers. When I was growing up my mom worked at the White House for President's Nixon, Ford, and Carter. After leaving the White House she went to work at Headquarters at PSI. My dad was in the media business and worked for the Washington Post for over 20 years and USA Today. He was also a consultant for the Washingtonian Magazine and BET.

It is imperative that I give you that background in order for you to be able to understand that I didn't come from a broken home, nor was I a neglected child. I came from a wonderful upbringing and I had great role models as parents. All of the tools that I needed to become successful at a very young age were in the palm of my hand, but I chose to follow my own accord. A lot of bad decisions were made in my early years that set me back on my journey towards greatness. Instead of planning for my future, I chose to run the streets. Partying, hanging out and drinking was my normal way of life. I was truly getting by from always finding something that I could hustle and make money off. I sold men's watches, fancy head scarfs, anything that I thought I could get trending I would sell it. I'm sure people would not have been surprised if I was selling bottle water on the corner. I'm a true hustler at heart! You could drop me off anywhere in the United States and I'm going to figure out how to make money and connections. Often times I got financial assistance from boyfriends and my parents because in their eyes I was trying to make things happen.

After graduating from high school, I never wanted to go to college. I always had a job, because I love having my own money. Now keeping the job was another story. It was hard to get up for work after partying every night of the week. Another issue that I had was taking orders from my supervisors. Often times the delivery would be rude and disrespectful due to their position title. I don't know why some people in certain positions feel like they can talk to you any kind of way. Once it seemed as though I had enough I would either quit or get fired. If I felt disrespected, then in my mind it was time to go anyway. Don't get me wrong, I did have a few jobs that I absolutely loved! I have worked at a day care, law firm, mental health organization, and a HIV & AIDS financial assistance organization. My last place of employment was in the Office of the President at Howard University. I got into a dispute with my supervisor, because I corrected her and pointed out how she was dead wrong. I'm sure you can imagine how that day ended. I was given my check, because it was payday & given a severance package. I was asked to leave & not come back. Believe it or not, I was happy to walk out! I decided that day that I never wanted to work a 9-5 job again! I'm proud to say that was 11 years ago. I have always had that go-getter drive and hustler mentality. The problem was that when I left out of the house my focus was not on capitalizing on the things and people that could've elevated me to the next level. Instead, I was focused on having fun and hustling whatever I could find to keep a little change in my pockets.

My fun was taking ecstasy pills. I did this regularly for over 15 years, while still trying to be a go-getter and being an independent thinker at the same time. I didn't understand at the time that this was tearing my insides up. In my mind I was happy, smiling and doing what I wanted to do, so I thought everything was all good. Let me give you an example of how this drug made me feel when I walked out of the door. I already felt put together on the inside out without the drugs, but the pill made me feel like I was Beyoncé stepping out of the door every single day! Contrary to popular belief, drug did not change my personality, appearance, or my positive spirit. One thing that I have always been was a happy and a family orientated person. If you were not in my personal social circle you would have never known unless I told you. In my mind I was fine, because when I looked in the mirror I looked great. When I was about 22 years old I first tried ecstasy. After the first time I was hooked. Being the happy person all day every day was who I was anyway. The pill made me feel like I was the happiest person in the entire world. What that drug did was enhance every sense of greatness that a person had within them to the 100th power. It got to the point that I would not leave out of the house to get my day started until I popped a pill. Through the course of the day I might have taken 2-4 pills in a day. It wasn't until 2008 did I get a wake-up call. That call sent my world tumbling down. My dad passed. I was supposed to be taking him to the hospital to have fluid drained from his stomach and taking him back home the same day. Instead something went wrong and he had to have emergency surgery. We were told that the surgery went well later that night. My family and I went home praying that we would be bringing dad home soon. What we never expected was getting a call and coming to the hospital to see my dad swollen all over and brain dead. My dad never came home with me as planned. He was dead the very next morning. In that moment I had never felt that much pain in my entire life. My heart was truly broken, because I not only lost my dad, I lost part of my heart. Realizing that I no longer had the man that raised me and loved me unconditionally, I felt like my life was over without my dad in it. I was strong to the world and an emotional, depressed wreck everyday behind closed doors. I felt like I had to stay strong because I had to be the backbone for my family now. The more I prayed, the more I started to hear my dad's words in my head guide me towards my greatness. He was tough and installed great values and life lessons into me. I made up my mind to make him proud all the way in heaven. He would let me have it if he could, about me just sitting around crying every day. My dad's spirit made me determined to start working on making myself a better person. I am a reflection of him.

Just when I was ready to do the right things for myself, I was hit with another bomb! I was diagnosed with high blood pressure & fibromyalgia. This was the moment that I decide that I had to get myself together and make the most out of my life.

Finally, having a clear understanding of the direction that I wanted to go in, I had to keep it moving even though there were times when I could barely move without a cane or assistance. Fibromyalgia is an auto immune disease. It attacks your nerves and triggers wide spread chronic pain throughout your body. Often times the pain is from my finger tips to my toes. After my dad passed there would be times that my mother would have to give me a bath because I couldn't move. She would also have to feed me or hold a cup of juice to my mouth as if I were her infant daughter again. I know it was a struggle for her, but she always stayed strong for me. My mom is truly my real-life Wonder Woman! Fibromyalgia can be triggered by stress, traumatic experiences and sometimes from absolutely nothing at all. So many people told me to just sit back and get disability. I told myself that as long as I could get up, walk and make moves that I would do it on my own. It might sound crazy, but our biggest supporters are GOD along with our "will and determination" to succeed. If you have a fire burning inside of you that won't go out, you can do whatever you set out to do in this world. I was determined to do just that!

Pushing through the pain with a smile, a few years later I had a mild stroke and doctor's discovered that I had a rare parasite that was eating away at my stomach and intestines. The parasite was actually eating me alive and I had no idea. The doctors told my family and I that it was a possibility that I would not make it to my next birthday if all the antibiotics that I was taking didn't work. Even still, I kept a positive frame of mind and kept my faith as I watched myself go from a size 7 to a size 1 in 4 months. Through it all I kept smiling, grinding and working on building my brand and own business relationships. I would have never been able to keep my spirits lifted if it were not for a hand full of my girlfriends calling me, making plans with me and praying with me daily. GOD worked out the rest, because in my heart and soul, I knew that it was a huge plan in the works for me. After taking 9 antibiotics a day for 14 days the healing process started to work. Even as of today I eat healthier and exercise regularly. Once again, the decision was made to work on me and keep pushing with a smile. At that point it was just me pushing me, there was no team. All I had was drive along with my determination to get out in the world and make difference. I started making my own moves and assisting others with making productive moves as well. A conscious decision was made that it was time to get my mind right 100 percent. I was no longer willing to give myself 80 percent, when I knew I was worth so much more. The first thing that I did was start talking to my GOD every single day. Something else that most people don't know about me is that years ago I did not believe in GOD. I thought there was a higher power and that's all I thought. I'm a lot wiser now. I always spoke life into my friends and family and I will forever be that shoulder for the people that I love during their toughest times in life. Through social media I started speaking life into others every day as well. I knew what I needed, so I knew there were people around me that needed to hear words of encouragement too. There are so many people full of greatness in the world that we live in. We just have to "Release the Debt" to be able to share our greatness with the world.

Believe it or not, I'm in my mid 40's now and I honestly feel as though I just started living my absolute best days. I could be bitter and fault myself for not making the best decisions in my 20's and early 30's, but I won't. Instead, I will continue to thank GOD for giving me the strength to keep pushing forward against all odds. If you are reading this and playing your own past over and over again in your mind, let it go! I am now a happy wife that is in business with an amazing and supportive husband with wonderful children that I'm so proud of. My family is just the best! My bond with my mom, brothers, nieces, nephews, cousins, aunts and uncle fill my heart with complete joy. GOD has even blessed me with the best husband and extended family that a woman could ever ask for! And if you haven't figured it out by now, I am a successful entrepreneur running multiple businesses of my own, as well as serving as a partner in my husband's company. My cup is overflowing – but I'm a conqueror! I am also a television and stage actress that has starred on major national television networks such as TV One and the ID Channel. Three of those roles were supporting roles and one was a leading role. My first stage acting debut was in August 19th, 2017 in the sold-out stage play "Decades." A year later on August 20, 2018, I was an actress in the national stage play musical "The GIZ" which was the very first stage play at the MGM National Harbor Casino and it was also a sold-out show of over 3,000 people! Who would have ever thought? I am often hired to host private and public events throughout the DC Metropolitan area. That job warms my heart because I love people and truly love uplifting others. In early 2018, I started my own jewelry line called "Ultimate Jewels." Not only do I sell unique pieces that I hand pick, I also create one-of-a-kind bracelet sets that women are going crazy over locally and nationally.

My true feeling of total accomplishment will be when I shake up the nation with my very first stage play that brings mental health and HIV awareness more to the forefront. I will not stop until that dream becomes reality! One thing I've learned in life is that you go hard or go home – aim so high that the vision scares you. So I am claiming that all things are possible and this dream of mine will come to fruition by this time in 2019. God has truly blessed me with placing some amazing people into my life that truly believe in me and my vision. I have had a lot of people that came on board with my vision and when it was time to take action they disappeared. I understand that GOD made that happen, so I'm no longer bitter or mad. What I received after that was reassurance by having Whitman Walker Health to come on board as my community partner. That was yet another sign from GOD that I am on the right path. My resources and connections are expanding more and more every day and that alone is a blessing in disguise. When it's my time, I promise the world that my stage play will save lives and open eyes at the same time. *GOD is working through me in a major way ...*

There are certain things that we should know about this life that we live. No matter how many mistakes that we have made, it's never too late to change your life around. The key to that is realizing that you need to change, and you want to change. We as people get caught up in moving forward and seeing ourselves on top over anything else. If you are not ready for success you will never reap the benefits of the longevity of success. Being ready is realizing that the change must start with you! Once you know where you want to go in life and what you want to do in life be obsessed with creating that life. Decide not to sell yourself short anymore by making reckless decisions. At the same time forgive yourself for those same reckless decisions. Remember that nobody is perfect, and we are all sinners. The good thing about is that every day that we are blessed to see another day we have a chance to better ourselves.

Stay focused on what is going to work for you in reference to crushing your goals and dreams. People often get caught up in the hype and limelight of what other people are doing to obtain their goals. That is a huge mistake that will only set you back or slow you down. The last thing that you want to do on your path to success is compare your journey to anyone else's. What other people are doing should be none of your business or concern. You cannot be a dream crusher worrying about or minding other people's business. Stay focused and don't rush your process. Your process will happen for you at the perfect time and not a soul on this planet can take it away from you once it happens. *What's for you is for you, and you only ...*

I could go on and on about how it's possible to turn your life around at any age or stage in your life, but through my story, I believe you can see the possibilities. You can be given all the tools and love that you need to reach your full potential, but if you are not ready to receive it, it won't matter. What does matter is that you free yourself from your past mistakes and setbacks. Look in the mirror and decide today that you want all the glory that your life has to offer you! Let it be no more fighting the demons in your mind of what could have been or should have been in your past. Focus solely on what you are going to do to make the best of the rest of your life from this day forward. My final words to you are to just "Release the Debt," if I can do it, so can you!

ABOUT THE AUTHOR

 **DANA HICKS-HUNGERFORD** is a native Washingtonian known for her very candid way of speaking and her willingness to always lend a hand to those in need.

She is the CEO of Ultimate Jewels LLC, a high-end lux jewelry company that specializes in custom-crafted stainless-steel bracelets. Her favorite pastime is acting and has been seen on the big screens of major networks like TV One, the ID Channel and Amazon TV. But it doesn't stop there! Dana has also made major waves on stage in several hit stage plays that included the sold out hit stage play *"Decades"* and *"The Giz"*, a spinoff of the legendary The Wiz, that paid homage to the great natives of Washington, DC. She will also be starring in the upcoming television series *"Loyal & Trust"* airing soon on Netflix.

Being a heavy advocate for community support, Dana is actively and consistently speaking to empower men and women on the importance of support and generating wealth together for the betterment of our children's legacy. She is a permanent influence in community outreach organizations such as Kaizen Life Skills, Boys 2 Bowties, Momma's Safe Haven and MoMedia LLC.

BEHIND EVERY SMILE THERE'S A STORY

Written by

Dawn Moss

I am a book. Containing knowledge that no one else can relate to or comprehend unless he or she takes the initiative to at least open me up, and then hear me out. I can take one through many emotional changes. I can make you cry when you are happy, laugh when you are sad. I can be mysterious, persuasive and even convincing when I am at my best but yet, according to your moods, I can somehow bend to reach those personalities that no one else has looked far enough to handle. I can be put on a shelf with others or stored away in isolation and still contain all my knowledge within me without discomfort or hesitation.

To be born Black is to be born a gifted child of the universe and I will survive always because I can face myself. You see, I am a groovy bird and the rhythm of my wings are endless. To the Black he's and she's that rose and rise like the sun over Africa, they were strong, proud and fearless we say…Peace to you all and long live those warriors in their search for liberation. They were soldiers for justice, freedom fighters, diamonds you are is we is love, is God, is poetry. God is God is Poetry. He is pure purity. He is naturally natural. He is life and laughter, song and dance. He is Holiday and Hathaway and oh how their hearts flew. So, on cloudy days when sunsets can't be seen remember what she meant when she pleaded God Bless the child or why he cried the blues although he was young, gifted and black.

It's so hard to be earth-bound when your wings are aching the high tide of the revolutionary wind. And it's real hard to remain terrestrial when your skin remembers being a bird and your heart soars back and forth in its own ribbed cage. That's me, that's we, that's love, that's God and this is poetry. LOL.

I get excited when I think about how far these words have gotten me since I was 16 years of age. I was born in Camden, New Jersey and raised is a small town named Sicklerville. Being the youngest of four hasn't been an easy task. I've always put pressure on myself to perform and in my way, I was trying to keep up with my siblings. Academically speaking, I struggled in school, almost failing a few times. I still have nightmares of not graduating and sometimes I must process my mind to remember," Wow, I received a full basketball scholarship to Morgan State University." Now that was different, because my high school was very diverse, and I never imagined that I would struggle socially the way that I did. I struggled academically, as well and oh not to mention the level of competition was very highly skilled.

My parents were typical old fashion southern people. My relationship with them was great. They were pretty strict but treated me like the baby I was. Some would say I was spoiled but I see things different especially when I would have to take whippings for things I've done wrong. My siblings didn't step in for those.

For the most part I was a good girl, just mischievous at times. My parents separated my freshman year in college, so I found myself going through somewhat of a depression. Playing basketball was my only outlet but somehow, I found myself feeling alone. My family was the go-to house in our neighborhood, so it really came as a surprise to most that they had split. I had become really good at isolating myself and hiding my true feelings from others.

I was able to cope by playing basketball, and my teammates became my family. I grew a close relationship with my teammate Dana and somehow the stability of her household and parents became my way of escape whenever I could spend time with them.

Growing up in the church has helped me a great deal. My church family was everything and still is. Those old school principles never leave you once they get deep down into your spirit. "Hold on to Gods Unchanging Hand, Peace Be Still, He's Sweet I Know, and the Blood that Jesus Shed for Me, became a few of my all-time favorite negro spirituals. I still sing them to this day whenever I feel down I think about the elders who would sometimes shout and cry out how good God is and now I finally can relate to the tears and praise. Believe me, it gets me through. He's the Dr. The Lawyer, the Teacher, The Redeemer, I mean when old school pastors would talk about Christ they would say everything that I didn't want to be. People never said He's the model, the actor, The hip-hop rapper… LOL. Those were some of the things I was striving to be. I told myself that I would search for the truth in the word and really figure out how I can be more Christ Like. So, I started seeing him in an entirely new light. I began to seek Gods face and goodness in everyone and everything I did. Peoples smiles, sparkling eyes, and good energy went a long way. I would listen to inspirational music and ministry, this change enabled me to empower myself to believe that God is truly everywhere.

There were two people that I met during my early years of college. My Image Maker Travis Winkey was introduced to me by some friends who knew he was a world-renowned fashion icon. I wanted to be a part, so I encouraged myself to walk into his studio one day and I was in awe of what I seen. Beautiful multicultural, environment of men and women who wanted to make it in fashion and in life. Travis and his assistant instructors helped me see that Modeling was an outlet that I could use to do everything I've dreamed in life. Little did I know that modeling would bring me closer to God. The second person was Dr. Lance London, who showed me that you could become great and live your dreams as far as you could see and beyond. In both cases, I never met anyone who spoke the way they did about life. I knew very early on that these two people would be in my life forever. I'm so glad about that. The impact that they made on my life was unlike anything I had ever experienced. They were both successful in their way. They were about building the African American community and making a difference in the lives of millions.

I got into Pageants totally by accident. Thorough modeling, and traveling, by working with Travis I was trained in many things. Posture, photography, runway, and self- care. In 1995 He became the State Director for Miss Black USA. Trying to be something that I am not, I wasn't really honest about the role I wanted to play in the Miss Black Maryland USA State Pageant, but I found myself very interested in learning more. Now mind you, I had still been going through bouts of depression since my parents divorced. I became a great actress, hiding my true feelings from everyone but I was able to cope most thinking about my elders who would say… Hold on to Gods unchanging hands. I even got involved with a few relationships that totally took me off track. Self-abuse can be tricky, and it can show up in many ways. I was meeting drug dealers, bank robbers, pimps and just straight out crazy fools. I was a sheep in a wolf's convention and I never imagined that I would find myself in a situation that I'd be fighting for my freedom and for my life. I had chosen friends who were up to no good and those individuals tried to trap me into a lifestyle of drugs, prostitution and exploitation. Nevertheless, I remembered the words of my Grandma who would always remind me to never let go.

Life is strange and I being the natural leader I am on the surface, I suffered inwardly and quietly not realizing that I was heading down a wrong path if I didn't get back to my roots.

One day I was driving home from work and I looked up. Mind you I had been travelling this same road every day and through my depression, I had not noticed the beautiful trees, birds, and homes, that surrounded me while on that path. I pulled over to the side of the road with tears of joy in my eyes and I began shouting…Thank you Jesus. I had an instant overwhelming feeling of joy and unlike my other counterparts who had died, been murdered, is swinging from a pole, and even locked up…I was still here. This revelation made me feel so good and I couldn't wait to express my new-found freedom to my friends, my family and to the world.

I immediately called my friend Kelly, who is the assistant to Travis Winkey, with tears of joy in my eyes I shared…" I want to compete in the Pageant." She immediately started laughing and said… "It's about time." We have been waiting for you to say this. We think you are the BEST candidate for the job." To my surprise, I couldn't believe it, so I immediately went to work. I prayed and said…" Lord, you said in your word if you believe and have faith you can do all things." My scripture became Faith is the substance of things hoped for and the evidence of things not seen.

My prayer is to become a role model like you. So, I started seeing Christ as the person I am striving to be. A model, a role model. He spoke in parables, so I made him a poet. He carried a cross, so I made the stage mine…And He enlarged my territory. I couldn't ask for anything more.

My road to competition couldn't have been more obvious that God's presence was all over it. I had been traveling across the country with television star Monique as her assistant and couldn't have asked for any more exposure that would give me the confirmation I needed to believe I could win. Oh yes, Christ traveled, and people wanted to know more about him, so I had opportunities to share with others that I was competing for the National title in a week.

My experience was great. While on tour, I received a call from a friend that there was a modeling job opportunity in the islands. I had been hustling and bustling, so I jumped at the chance to get away. I drove 13 hours from Atlanta Georgia to catch a flight from Washington, DC to St. Kitts.

While sitting on the runway I started thinking about my grandmother, the late Estella Artis, who I based my talent as her character for the competition. She was the first person in my life who had died while I was in college who I knew I really loved. I remember my mother, sharing with me the story of her death and compared how beautiful her transition was from our world to heaven. She compared it to the airplane ride and how her spirit just took off up in the air. She said there was a beautiful glow that took over her body and that she looked as if she was sleeping on a cloud. Since I was not at the hospital in NJ when she passed, I decided that I would take myself through the experience of her transition.

Oh Grandma, I miss you so much.

The plane took the runway, and began to pick up speed, I was in awe of how well my mom had described her home-going transition. I was up in the air now and I found myself in full conversation with God. I began to asking questions. Lord, how was Grandma's transition? Then immediately a cloud drifted pass with a face of a person as if they were resting on a pillow. I couldn't believe my eyes. Now I need to remind you that I asked God to take this walk with me because I wanted to be exactly like Him.

As I sat frozen in my seat, I started to play a mental game. I was looking at the clouds and identifying the characters. That's a bear, that's a clown, that's a car, I mean God was playing a game with me and it was at that point that I realized he had a sense of humor.

Lord you're a comedian. That' s when I heard the sound of His sweet voice. To me it got louder and louder. I around on the plane thinking that everyone could hear what He was saying, only to realize that I was the only one. Emotionally, I started crying. I used to think Gods voice was loud and bold like we would hear on television. TV would scare you to death. MOSES, Where ART THOU? LOL.

Moving on, I still played my game and I got to a shape that I couldn't figure out. I started seeing them everywhere. All I heard was God say… "Dawn remember this experience." Writing about it chokes me up because this is a promise I am fulfilling. Isn't He awesome?

Pageant week came so fast and I could hardly contain my excitement. Lincoln Theatre that night was about to be filled with people from all over the country. Competition was tight because the talent and the poise and beauty of these women was impeccable.

I remember walking in the theatre and going upstairs to the balcony seats. I wanted to see it from a view of the audience and my family members that would be arriving soon. It's rare that black families get together for things other than funerals, so I was elated that so many of my family members were coming to see little old me.

I gave Jesus a seat up there and I told Him if I was to get nervous, I'd look up and know he's in the room. That was enough for me, so I went back stage to get ready.

Anything that could go wrong did that day. My clothes were not there yet so I was thinking I had to simply wear the items I was wore in preliminaries. I had to keep a positive attitude. Lucky for me, it was my turn to sit in the make-up chair. Derrick Rutledge was my guy and I asked him to create on me the winners face. He did just that. Seconds before it was time for us to enter the stage my clothes appeared. *Thank You Lord.*

Coming out was amazing and before I did my introduction I looked up into the balcony where I gave Christ a seat and there to my surprise was the spotlight. It was so warm and bright it looked just like the sun. I knew right away, I was exactly where I needed to be, and Jesus was in the building.

My first words were Faith is the essence of things hoped for and the evidence of things not seen. Every time I came out I looked up and God took over. I was excited. Like Christ had 12 disciples, I was #12. I couldn't believe it and I was oblivious to everything that was going on around me.

Ok so now we get to the end of the completion when the announcements would be made. I remember standing there talking to God again and saying, "Here we are…" The announcer said … 5th runner up … Miss Alabama!

In my mind I was like ok Lord, you said in your word if you believe and have faith all things are possible. I believed, and you already called the 5th runner ups name. The announcer then said…4th runner up…. Miss Mississippi!

In my mind I said ok Lord I changed my ways, I tried my best and I'm not even 4th runner up? What's up?

The announcer proceeded to call 3rd runner up, 2nd runner up … 1st runner up … and I was not among those that were called. By then I was livid. I was mad at God and started questioning all my experiences in the clouds, the run-way, the plane … I even questioned the seat I gave him. Whew! Then something came over me, there is something about the name of Jesus. I caught myself and snapped out of my pity party. I instead began to thank him and praise Him for all that He's done in my life this far. He Lord spared my life from the streets, He saved me, He changed me, He molded me, and shaped me. He picked me back up to where I have always wanted to be. My family and my friends are here. My mentors are here and so was God. I am grateful. Whatever your will is, let it be done, and as soon as I said those words, Christ, I felt like I took my last breath, and that's when the announcer said …

The winner and new Miss Black USA 1996 is … Miss Black Maryland Dawn Moss!

My journey has been one of teaching, traveling, mentoring, and assisting others in building their brand. I love what I do because so many doors continue to open. I even became executive producer for Miss Black USA for five years, beginning my journey in Gambia, West Africa. My proudest moments were changing the way the Gambia views television and bring to rival tribes together in unity after centuries of fighting since Kunta Kinte error.

Behind every smile there is story. The Bible speaks of many Queens and Wise Women. These ladies give us strong references that can encourage those of us who want to be virtuous and please God. Truth is, we want to be powerful and beautiful like the Queens who are referenced in the Bible. My question to you is …Which Queen do you resemble? My mother Beatrice P. Artis Ray for example, has set a new standard on what it truly means to be a virtuous woman. There was a time in my life when I wanted to forget my past, and all the choices that I made that did not please God. My mom taught me to face myself so today I stand on the shoulders of those choices I made, and I am stronger because of them. This is what I love about God. He makes all things new. I will forever speak on those golden memories and embrace the power that the Lord gives us all to get up and rise above our circumstances. Get excited. Let's walk with pride, and dignity into your prosperous future that God has planned for our life. Wisdom is the bridge between knowledge and understanding. Stand. Say to yourself, I love my future and I am a better me because of my past. Keep the Faith. And remember to hold on to Gods unchanging hands.

My sash came first. By his stripes I am healed. My crown was placed on my head … They were not thorns … They were Diamonds. Thank You Jesus, I will continue to REIGN ON!"

ABOUT THE AUTHOR

DAWN MOSS is the Founder and CEO of Good Girls Getting Better Empowerment Forum and Executive Managing Partner for Big City Foods LLC – home of the Carolina Kitchen Restaurant chain.

She served as the former co-host for Baltimore Channel 2 ABC show *See America* and catapulted her media career by writing for several media publications as well as serving as the producer of CNN 1010 network program.

Solidifying the winning title of "Miss Black USA" in 1996, Dawn used her education and experiences to impact the lives of many by volunteering her time and service to many churches and non-profits globally.

THE JOURNEY HOME

Written by

Tatonya Holman

Have you ever lost a loved one? Have you ever questioned why God would take your loved one away? Have you ever thought about how you would move on without that person? We all know that God gives us the gift of life, but one day your earthly life will end.

My 2017 journey was one that I could not have ever imagined ...

As a little girl, I remember my parents always being present. We grew up middle class, my dad was a pastor, educator and worked extremely hard. My mom was a registered nurse, and a stay-at-home mom for all our childhood years. My parents attended every basketball game, track meet and extracurricular activity that we were involved in. We were raised in a strict Christian home. There was lots of love, and my dad was overly affectionate as he always hugged and kissed us frequently. We attended church every Sunday, no excuses. They were truly the model parents, and the biblical principles and foundation that was laid for us afforded us a blessed life that instilled values that would help me navigate this journey of ***Living Intentionally with Faith and Expectancy (L.I.F.E.)*** The Bible says that the life of human flesh begins with birth and ends at death. God tells us that He sent His Son so that we may not just have life, but that we may have it more ABUNDANTLY! Having a very strong Christian foundation, I was very clear that living here on earth was temporary, and everyone must transition one day. We knew that how we lived our lives on earth would dictate our final destination. I didn't realize until recently, that what was poured into me would get me through some difficult days that would change the trajectory of my life.

On a beautiful day in June of 2015, I was on a business trip in Norfolk, Virginia when I received a call that would forever change my life. Even three years later, I still remember the call so vividly. You know that feeling when something life changing happens, you always know exactly where you were and what you were doing? This was that kind of moment. I come from a very close-knit family, so I spoke to my parents often; but there was something different about this call. Daddy requested that my sisters and I join a three-way call with him so he could give us some important news. I could hear in his voice that something was wrong. When I answered the phone, I remember my dad speaking words that no daughter wants to hear. He said, "Tonya are you by yourself? I responded "Yes." He made sure my two sisters were also on the phone. He proceeded to say the words "I have been diagnosed with cancer" ... my heart literally stopped, and I couldn't find the words to respond. Those six words took my breath away as I sat on the phone quietly trying to collect myself to think of a response. Before I could respond, I heard daddy's voice say, "I am going to be just fine and I will fight this, so please don't worry, just pray for healing." After hanging up the phone, I distinctly remember having a conversation with GOD asking him to please heal my dad and do it immediately!

After the cancer diagnosis, we met as a family to discuss the options. He wanted to make sure that we knew exactly what "we" were up against, and he was committed to us being a part of this journey. After meeting with the medical staff and having an extensive review of his situation, daddy made the decision to have surgery. Naturally, we were very nervous, but we rest assured that he would be just fine. I remember the day I traveled to Pennsylvania to be with my mom on surgery day. She was a bundle of nerves but was truly believing in his healing. She was the type of woman that always stood steadfast in her faith. Several weeks after the surgery, we met with the specialists and they announced he was "cancer free". *What a celebration!* We could finally breathe knowing he was on his way back to normal. God answered our prayers.

About a year later, we received another unexpected call from my dad. He said, "the cancer is back." Of course, this news was shocking! A wave of questions flooded my mind. How could this happen? I was angry, confused frustrated, just so many emotions, as I didn't understand why God was allowing him to suffer this way. This man was the patriarch of the family, someone everyone relied on. So here we are again meeting with the medical staff, specialized doctors and having various consultations, as we contemplated our options. We decided the best treatment for the time around would be the holistic route, which meant all-natural remedies such as vitamin C injections and changing to a plant-based diet. Over the next year, between treatments and therapy, my life was committed to helping my mother care for him and relieve her whenever she needed. As time passed, he became weaker and soon was forced to make a decision to take some time away from pastoring to focus on his health. This was a very difficult decision for him. He loved his church and having the constraints of not being able to be in his element was a challenge.

Every other weekend for months, my sister and I traveled to my hometown to help relieve my mom. I used the car ride as a sacred place to pray and to build a stronger connection to God. My conversations with God were serious, and I was struggling with why my family had to deal with this ordeal. I asked God to spare his life over and over, but I also didn't have a choice but to think about how our lives would change if he was taken from us. I felt horrible thinking about life after daddy, but I stood on God's word.

Romans 6:23
For the wages of sin is death, but the gift of God is eternal life in Christ Jesus our Lord.

God calls all believers to fight in spiritual battles that are constantly taking place, where evil causes suffering, but God works to redeem it for good purposes. We had some praying warriors in our circle and now was the time for me to reach out to them for support and get serious with my prayer life. It was time to put on the spiritual armor that my daddy always preached about. We were under spiritual attack. I needed God to heal him. We could not lose him. Prayer is the portal that brings the power of heaven down to earth. I immersed myself with prayer strategies to make sure that they were getting through. I started reading lots of structured prayers and even using my closet as a place of refuge to really call out to God. I focused all my energy on praying for him. Every waking moment, I prayed. Through intentional and strategic prayer, you must tell Jesus everything. Prayer is the fuel that drives everything. We called our entire circle of family and friends to join us in corporate prayer. For months, everyone prayed and fasted for his healing. Surely, he was going to be okay, and back preaching very soon. I felt a sense of peace knowing that we had people of faith believing he would again overcome. He will live and shall not die!

It seemed like every other day my mom would text or call us with an update of his progress. There were quite a few setbacks, and I kept telling myself that the comeback must be on the way. The stress we endured was crippling. Every time the phone rang, I could feel my blood pressure going up. This roller coaster lasted for months. Not only was I worried about my dad, but very concerned about my mom who carried a huge burden. Her life was completely consumed making sure he was getting the best care. Yet again, I questioned God why he was going through this. I would ask him during our many conversations, "daddy, why do you think God chose you, to suffer," and he would say "Why not me?" His response caused me to pause. Here he was not even frustrated or angry for all the pain that he was enduring. He would say, "I am the chosen one, and look at what Jesus went through and for some reason God chose me to suffer." This was so hard for me to accept, because I hated seeing my dad in excruciating pain and deteriorating as time passed. This was a man who used his life to bring souls to serve the kingdom. Certainly, God still had work for him to do. I exercised my faith daily believing that he was going to be fine. I knew what it meant to be faithful, and I knew God used situations to create a deeper faith where we totally must rely on him. This was the moment where I had to surrender all and be okay with God's will.

Hebrews 11:1
Now faith is the substance of things hoped for,
the evidence of things not seen.

In May 2017, in addition to dealing with my dad's health challenges, I was also dealing with a crisis. I underwent major surgery that took me to a very dark place. My plan was to have the surgery and be on the mend in about eight weeks. Well, my plan didn't happen the way I expected. After surgery, and dealing with post-surgery complications, I suffered. My life changed in an instant. I was wearing a colostomy bag that was not only uncomfortable but very embarrassing and was told by my specialist that I had to wear adult diapers because of the continuous bladder issues. I would go days without getting out the bed because of the pain and the sadness I felt. My husband and kids literally were taking care of me, and it was difficult to rely on them for everything. I hated not being able to fend for myself. I would pray and ask God, why I was going through this. He would whisper "It's not about You." What did he mean? It's not about me? I am here struggling to get better, and he says, "It's not about you." You talk about attitude, and a serious one I had. My dad would call me religiously during this time amid his challenges to encourage me and to pray for me. My mom said he would lose sleep because he was worried about me. Wow! Imagine this is a man who was in extreme pain 90 % of the time who found the strength to check on me, while I was feeling sorry for myself. (This was a perfect example of selflessness).

After a couple of weeks of feeling sorry for myself, I woke up one day and said "girl, you need to get it together." How in the world does my dad manage to have the strength to pray for me with all the issues he was going through? This was an "aha" moment, and I came to the realization quick that it wasn't about me after all and I needed to get up and praise my way through it. I exercised my inner strength and used my faith that was imparted and trusted that God was going to miraculously heal me, so I could get back to helping my parents. During my sickness, I was amazed that the challenges I was dealing with were very similar to what my dad was experiencing. God chose me to understand just a little bit of what he was going through, so I could appreciate that sometimes suffering is necessary. Finally, after a couple of months of my recovery, God "miraculously" healed my body. I was able to get back on the road to see my dad for the first time in months. His excitement to see me warmed my heart.

When I declared 2017 to be the year of *"preparation",* I couldn't even imagine what the year would bring. Being the oldest sibling, I believed my dad thought I could handle conversations about death. As I reflect, he was preparing me for his transition and the time I spent with him was an opportunity for us to create an even stronger bond. Our many hours of conversations helped me understand him in a way that strengthened our relationship. Priceless!

Daddy often talked about heaven and revealed to me that he wasn't sure how long he would be around. It was made very clear that he was also preparing himself to transition from this earth. He expressed that God provided him with a life most could only imagine and was blessed to see his three girls reach success and raise his grandchildren in a manner that made him proud. Hearing him talk like this warmed my spirit but made me a little sad at the same time knowing his time was winding down. He was my rock, my biggest support, my true hero. I could not imagine life without him.

On October 27, 2017, my beloved daddy transitioned. It was on this day that pain and sorrow consumed me. And while I had time to prepare, my heart broke in a million pieces. The pain I felt was indescribable and I wish for no one to feel this kind of pain. Yes, I know that to be absent from the body is to be present with the LORD. I knew he was no longer tired or suffering. I know! I am well aware of these truths, but you can't tell me that time heals all wounds. This was not the time! I was such in a place of despair. I instantly missed everything about him!

After weeks of trying to grasp that he will no longer be around, I tried to get back to a sense of normalcy and I realized I was stuck. I couldn't fathom not being able to hear his voice saying, "I Love You." Although, he tried to prepare me for his transition, it was very hard for me to come to terms. It was difficult to get out of bed. I disguised my pain very well because I didn't know how to cope with it. My closest friends and family would call and check on me, and ask how I was doing, and I always answered, "I am fine," but deep down I was hurting. One day I woke up and said to myself, "I have to deal with this grief." As a strong woman, I felt that I should be able to get back up and return to my normal. I was crazy to think this! This was not okay. What I discovered was that we need time to grieve when we lose a loved one. As strong as I thought I was, I was forced to take the time to heal.

When it comes to life after death, I am no expert, but what I do know is that there is no shame in taking time to process. The grieving process is one that cannot be rushed - it has not time limit. When you have someone in your life for such a long time, you need to take the time and grieve the way you need to. It's a process and my advice is to surround yourself with people who can uplift and encourage you. Get counseling if you need to talk to someone. Depression is real, and I am grateful for the support of my circle and the encouragement I received. I realized it's what I do in the space and time given that will facilitate the healing. Every day, I have a choice. I have the option of feeling sorry for myself and not process my feelings, or I can choose to do something different; I could choose to open myself up to the healing process and allow grief to do what only it can do. I've learned over the last few months that there are times in our lives when healing is an intentional choice. Life can't stop when you lose a loved one.

It was something about my dad's transition that ignited me to live bolder and braver. I developed a deeper relationship with God. I have more compassion and empathy for people. I truly understand the power of giving. I forgive without thinking about it, I have peace that surpasses all understanding, and loving my enemies is seamless. Freedom is a wonderful feeling! Discovering my own strength with the loss of my dad has been powerful. I always knew that my life would be bigger than I could ever imagine. I am using his life as my example, to serve and give more. God is using every bit of what my family has gone through as a testimony bringing pain to purpose. I am trusting God to not only bring us through this pain but renew us to be stronger than before.

Exodus 20:12

Honor your father and mother that your days may be long upon the land which the Lord your God is giving you.

So many lessons from this journey that I can apply to my life. I truly understand my divine purpose. Although your loved one may not be with us physically they are with us spiritually. I am guided by his faith, convictions and a desire to live a life that is pleasing to God and that would be an example for my kids to follow.

God places us in this world to make an impact. What a beautiful way to live! Living with significance, passion and an unwavering faith that can't be shaken is a true gift. Keeping God, Faith and Family at the forefront is necessary, and it's so important to place boundaries around your sacred place. I often asked myself, "What more can I do to impact the lives of others?" He gives me an answer every time.

Surround yourself with people that uplift you and encourage you to live out your best life and know you can experience joy after death. The one thing I am grateful for is that I cherished my dad while he was here. My soul rests easy knowing I said everything I needed to say. Ask yourself a question, "If your loved one passed away today, did you say and do everything you wanted to do?" Remember, life is short and it's not about our time, but about God's perfect timing, so *live* each day with purpose.

With God's grace, my family is finding a way to move forward. We are at peace knowing that we were richly blessed to have him for 73 years. He taught me so much goodness that will allow me to let my light shine unapologetically while using my gifts to impact others. Everything my dad poured into me will help me to live a life of be significance and fulfillment.

Trust me this process has not been easy, but I can honestly say I am eternally grateful to wake up every morning with another opportunity to make a difference. I don't take life for granted. I know we sometimes question God as to why our loved ones must leave us, especially when they have endured suffering. We must accept that

God gives us life, and uses life for the betterment of people, and God also takes life for betterment of his kingdom. God has a better plan beyond our understanding. God will use the death of someone close to you for good.

Decide to live (L.I.F.E.) Living Intentionally with Faith and Expectancy.

Romans 8:28
All things work together for good for those who love the Lord and has been called according to his purpose.

ABOUT THE AUTHOR

TATONYA HOLMAN is a speaker, co-author, wellness strategist with a purpose to *Strengthen, Empower,* and *Encourage* excellence in all aspects of the lives of young girls and women through outreach programs and global events.

Her passion for empowering women and positively impacting and changing lives is the catalyst of her mission. She uses her wealth of knowledge in the health and wellness industry to educate people on shifting the way they think about their health and wellness by offering personal health consultations to aid them on their journey.

As Founder and Chief Executive Officer of *Women of Excellence (W.O.E).* a 501(c)3 foundation that assists homeless and battered women in re-establishing themselves and their families in the local communities, she serves as the voice of empowerment through forums and conferences for youth and women throughout the DC/Maryland area.

Her sincere prayer is that the community we serve be armed with life application principles to inspire all women from all walks of life walk and love in "Excellence".

Learn more about this author at www.tatonyaholman.com

HEALING HISTORY

Written by

Brandy Tookes

I was born Brandy Tookes, a native of the island of Trinidad and Tobago. In an unfortunate but so familiar story from my childhood, my hope is that my transparent history will encourage others to get back on track to their destiny.

If I were to conduct a survey using everyone reading this chapter and ask, *"Have you ever been sexually assaulted or harassed?"* One might be surprised of how largely positive the outcome will be. Studies by the Crimes Against Children Research Center, show that 1 in 5 girls, and 1 in 20 boys are a victim of child sexual abuse (CSA).

Sexual abuse by a relative is a significant part of the problem. According to statistics from RAINN.org every eight minutes a child is sexually assaulted in the US, and 93% know the perpetrator. Many perpetrators of sexual abuse are in a position of trust or responsible for the child's care such as a family member, teacher, clergy member or coach. Such statistics are emblematic of an epidemic, but as a society we haven't given these cases much attention in the past. It's easy to push something aside when it isn't staring us in the face and, typically, crimes of a sexual nature are hidden away. There's shame pushed on to the victims and those in power are given the ability to hide their vile sides. Recently, there has been a push for victims to have their voices heard. Victims are taking back their power and no longer allowing silence to be forced upon them. But the battle is still very much an upward one.

In America – and around the world – this issue deserves a lot more attention in order to eradicate it. The

Caribbean, where am I am from, is a slice of this earth that finds itself in recent years, standing up efforts to educate families, schools, and communities on how to protect our innocent children. For me, experiencing childhood sexual abuse while growing up in Trinidad in the 80's and 90's did not include such savvy reporting or support systems. Because of my DNA, I was born into the vicious cycle of holding my brokenness and hurt inside. There was no outlet provided, no therapist to talk, and for a while, no family to lean on. The pain I carried was supposed to follow me to the grave – till death do us part. My mother, my grandmother, and the countless women in my family were a part of the same tradition of maintaining the secrecy: What goes on in this house, stays in this house. However, I have begun the work to end the cycle of this silent killer called childhood sexual abuse that has such ripple effects on so many families around world.

However, I am a living testimony that my history as a victim of sexual abuse can be healed and be used as a launching pad into my God given destiny.

I remember, around the age of 7, being a very skinny, happy-go-lucky girl always focused on the simple things of life: playing with my friends, my 5 brothers and cousins. We grew up in my grandmother's house that even though it was small, and I shared a bed with two other brothers, we had everything we needed including a ½ acre of land filled with an assortment of fruit trees and space to use our imagination to play. I also remember a very close cousin, Ted, not to excuse his behavior, but I know he must have been going through those early teenage hormones.

Sexual thoughts and urges possibly appearing to him for the first time, he decided he wanted to know what a vagina felt like. So why not touch the vagina, that slept in the same bedroom with her brothers. I woke up and asked, "what are you doing?" Ted shocked and scared but quickly said "nothing, are you having a bad dream?" I told my mother the next morning when I collected my thoughts and knew for a fact that I was not having a bad dream. She confronted Ted, verbally reprimanded him and that was that. I remembered sleeping with pants on from that point on and moved my sleeping spot against the wall so if he wanted to try again he'd have to reach over my brothers.

A couple years later my mother's boyfriend Wayne T. Kunley moved in our house. My siblings and I had mixed feelings because we all knew our biological father and even though he didn't do much for us at the time, we did not understand why this adult man had to begin living with us and was now allowed to set rules for us to follow and discipline us. My mother got a part time job and soon we were left home alone with Wayne. I became accustomed to hearing "Brandy bring in the broom and sweep."

"Brandy, didn't you hear me calling you?"

"Your mother wanted me to show you this."

"How does that feel?" "Make sure you don't tell anyone about this."

I remember walking into the dark room with the broom and dust pan in hand, being confused because I felt it was wrong, but he had my mother's permission, I remembered being nine years old and I hated my mother. I never understood why my mother would want me to know about *that* so young. I never understood why she had given him permission. I never understood any of it. I remember my brothers being mean because that's what brothers do especially as teenagers. I remember wanting to take my life. I hated everything – my life, the things happening to me, half of my family. I felt alone in a house filled with people. I didn't tell anyone, but I became this quiet girl who had lost her happy-go-lucky, free spirit. I began spending time by myself and at an early age learned to bury feelings by carrying on with life. Eventually, I found happiness in hanging out with my friends who were doing normal teenage things so that was therapy for me; I looked forward to times spent with friends because it made me forget about my home life.

I remember, at the age of 11, passing the Common Entrance Exam that advances students in Trinidad to the equivalent of middle school. It was registration day for my new school at Chaguanas Junior Secondary School and it was raining. My mother was home sleeping and believed I could register myself once I had all the pertinent documents with me. Well I did not have all the right documents and I had to go home, wake her up, get the required document and go back to the school. While I waited for her to find the documents, sadness and neglect overcame me because the other kids had their parents with them and mine was home nestled asleep to the soothing sounds of rain hitting the galvanized roof. I was walking back to catch a taxi and my neighbor – John, he was 40 or so, married with children

– was kind enough to offer me a ride. Not wanting to be in the rain any longer, I accepted. Little did I know, John saw it as an opportunity to make the invitation to his office for drinks and a "good time." I felt very uncomfortable and disgusted that this old man would think it was okay to invite me, a little girl in comparison to his old age, for drinks. I remembered being scared but smart enough to appear as if I was entertaining his invitation in thought by saying "okay, I'll think about it," so I can safely be dropped off at my school.

Starting this new school was different. I had new friends who were normal and focused on school, sisterhood, hair and rehearsing moves for our dance group. These served as an outlet for me. I had a class called Home Economics that for the first time taught me about sex education and all those blurry questions I had when I was younger became clear. I knew what had happened a few years prior was wrong. I had words to match my feelings. I made a vow to end this cycle of hurt by breaking the long-maintained silence. One day I was sitting on the porch with my second brother Don and in a heavy accent and my low voice, I said "Don I have something to tell you, but you promise not to tell anyone, okay?" I chose to confide in my second brother because he was always strong and stood for what was right. He used to be a bit of a hot head and I should have known he was going to do something about what I was about to say next. When I told him what had happened with Wayne, I remember his big eyes got bigger and loudly asked "why didn't you tell mummy?" "Because she told him to do it!" I said. His eyes grew even bigger. And that was it! Immediately, there was a big fight in the house. Don approached Wayne to fight him and my mom not knowing exactly what was going on got in the middle to break it up. Everything was starting to descend into chaos. My mom's friend, Anne, happened to be visiting at the time. I remember her calm and caring spirit pulled me aside from the chaos and asked me what was going on. Feeling comfortable to speak because of her calm and sincere caring voice, I told her what had transpired. That very day, I went away to an aunt in San Fernando, the southern part of Trinidad nothing out of the norm as I usually travelled there for the weekends to go to church. The trip came with a strict warning not to open my mouth. I adhered to the warning and when I returned home, Wayne had moved out. My mom had an attitude with me for a few days and then life went on from there. The cycle of secrecy continued once again.

For years, my experience of childhood sexual abuse went buried with life, in both conversation and emotion. It never came up. As a young adult in my twenties, I was able to date, have relationships and eventually became married. However, I experienced problems in my marriage that are statistically linked to long term effects from being a victim of child sexual abuse including trust, feelings of inadequacy, achieving deeper levels of intimacy and low self-esteem that stretched into relationships with friends, loved ones and even my career. I loved my husband very much and knew that I was his one and only but couldn't help believing that I wasn't good enough or beautiful enough. I especially struggled with being a mother; I vowed to never let the child sexual abuse cycle repeat itself my kids, yes, I vowed to break the cycle. By the time my kids knew to walk and talk they knew that their private parts were never to be touched by anyone except a doctor and only if mommy or daddy was there with them. They knew that they could always come to me or dad immediately if anyone touches their private areas or has any other sexual contact with them. After the age of 6 or 7 my daughter was no longer allowed to be tickled by anyone or sit on anyone's lap. My poor kids were not allowed to go to anyone's houses until I met the parents and had all sorts of awkward conversations with the sole purpose of silently screening their life for any signs that my child may be sexually abused if I left them there. I sat through birthday parties where I was the only parent who stayed back while other parents were happy for the few hours of alone time. I realized I had unresolved issues after I had an anxiety attack when my dad and his wife offered to take the kids for two weeks in the summer and my husband begged me to let them go so that we can have some alone time. Having studied in the medical field, my dad understood what I was experiencing, apologized for what I had experienced in his absence and even though he reassured me that the kids would be fine, I called every day and using code words that we created, the kids reassured me that they had not been sexually violated.

Even though my mother and I had a functioning mother-daughter relationship, it was fragmented with pieces of resentment for her lack of responsiveness and care towards me during my earlier years. One day we were talking about why I refused to allow my children to stay with her overnight. With a lot of anger in my voice and blurred vision, I verbally transferred the hurt that I carried, blaming her as the cause for my issues stemming from being sexually abused and reminded her that she didn't even apologize. I reminded her that I felt sad, betrayed and neglected on the day of school registration, because she left me vulnerable to it happening again. I asked her why did she let Wayne do that to me and her response broke my heart. For years we both acted like that day I broke my silence never occurred. My mom softly said, "I didn't know he was doing those things Brandy and I didn't know how to handle it once you said something, so I left it alone." Furthermore, she solidified that it was a cycle of hurt because her mother left her at an early age to travel abroad for work and she too was sexually abused. For the first time my mom, despite being filled with shame and guilt, apologized. I accepted her apology because I believe she did not know and an apology was all I wanted to hear.

As for our kids, thankfully, they are now 15 and 14 years old, and from time to time, I still ask them if anyone have made an inappropriate sexual comment or sexual contact. I also remind them that we are here for them if anything like that ever happens. Together my husband and I gradually began allowing our kids to stay with a select few trusted friends and family members who understand my past emotional wounds. I have learned that it is okay to use good judgment to trust people.

During a one-year period in the U.S., 16% of youth ages 14 to 17 had been sexually victimized. Children are most vulnerable to CSA between the ages of 7 and 13. Yes unfortunately these numbers are true, however, I am convinced that with continued efforts to educate, combined with greater emphasis on reporting and the recent movements to break the silence, that these numbers will gradually decline.

The advice I will give any parent on how to prevent child sexual abuse is to ensure you have situational awareness and have a presence. Being present for our kids both physically and in conversation to understand what their normal looks, sounds and feels like. This way when something, such as your child's mood, demeanor, or energy, changes you are aware enough to ask the right questions. Being present in conversation is having genuine dialogue with your child from adolescent thru teenage years and beyond so that you can relate to each other, and they will know without a shadow of a doubt that they have someone who will support them 100% if they are being sexually victimized. Yes, parents also be aware of who will be around your child in your absence simply by asking the question.

For community members, care givers, teachers and any advocate against child sexual abuse, I offer that you increase awareness about reporting across state lines to enable effective background checks. I offer that multiple layers of supervision be implemented to include monitored cameras and visible changing stations at day cares.

Talk about body parts early. Be candid with young kids when naming body parts. Use proper names for body parts, or at least teach your child what the actual words are for their body parts. Feeling comfortable using these words and knowing what they mean can help a child talk clearly if something inappropriate has happened.

Teach them that some body parts are private. Tell your child that their private parts are called private because they are not for everyone to see. Explain that mommy and daddy can see them naked, but people outside of the home should only see them with their clothes on. Explain how their doctor can see them without their clothes because mommy and daddy are there with them and the doctor is checking their body.

Teach your child body boundaries. Tell your child matter-of-factly that no one should touch their private parts and that no one should ask them to touch somebody else's private parts. Parents will often forget the second part of this sentence. Sexual abuse often begins with the perpetrator asking the child to touch them or someone else.

Tell your child that body secrets are not okay. Most perpetrators will tell the child to keep the abuse a secret. This can be done in a friendly way, such as, "I love playing with you, but if you tell anyone else what we played they won't let me come over again." Or it can be a threat: "This is our secret. If you tell anyone I will tell them it was your idea and you will get in big trouble!" Tell your kids that no matter what anyone tell them, body secrets are not okay and they should always tell you if someone tries to make them keep a body secret.

Technology has its place where sick pedophiles love to take and trade pictures of naked children online. This is an epidemic and it puts your child at risk. Tell your child that no one should take pictures of their private parts. This one is often missed by parents. There is a whole sick world out there of pedophiles.

Teach your child how to get out of scary or uncomfortable situations. Some children are uncomfortable with telling people "no"— especially older peers or adults. Tell them that it's okay to tell an adult they must leave, if something that feels wrong is happening, and help give them words to get out of uncomfortable situations. Tell your child that if someone wants to see or touch private parts they can tell them that they need to leave to go potty.

Forgiveness was the first step to my healing. I remembered feeling a bit emotionally lighter and somewhat relieved that my mother was not a person to hate; she too was betrayed by Wayne's actions. After this point, I began seeking therapy with a professional counselor because the old adage of "hurt people hurt people" was showing itself through the way I emotionally distanced myself from people and didn't understand how to love people who was trying to love me. I did not want this to be part of my legacy and it had to start with forgiving my mother and myself.

Counseling was the second step of my healing. Through counseling, I saw the distorted view of myself as an adult and was able to remove the false perception of I am not good enough or beautiful enough to now view myself in a healthy reality. I now view myself as being filled with God's love, peace and beauty.

Reshaping my thinking was the third step. Breaking free from the emotional debt that I incurred over the years was a decision I made with the support of my counselor, husband and especially one of my signature scriptures Romans 12:2 "and do not be conformed to this world but be transformed by the renewing of your mind." As a child sexual abuse victim, I decided that I can no longer allow my predators to rob me from having a bonded relationship with my mother, robbing our kids from having a regular teen-life or from allowing me to be the bold, brilliant, bodacious woman that I was created to be. I began reshaping my thinking and speaking positive affirmations that helped transformed the way I was thinking.

I also began realizing that I have become resilient and because of the affirmations I speak, my self-esteem and confidence are now where they need to be in order for me to leap into my destiny. Yes, history had to be healed so that I could be transformed into the woman I am today.

BRANDY "BEE" TOOKES is passionate about helping others "grow" around life's obstacles thru Romans12:2. Her goal is to provide life and career coaching services to help others transform into the best version of themselves. After finding freedom from adolescent sexual abuse, she seeks to inspire others towards their own transformation.

With over 15 years of HR experience, Brandy holds a master's degree in Human Resources Management, and works with the Department of Navy both as a government employee and the U.S. Navy Reserves as a Human Resources Officer.

She lives in Waldorf, MD with her husband and two wonderful children.

THE GIFT IN THE POWER TO OVERCOME

Written by

LaTalya Palmer

I can introduce myself as a fatherless daughter and incest survivor; a divorcee and single mom; a daughter grieving her mother's death; I can even introduce myself as a breast cancer patient but today I am going to introduce myself as LaTalya Monique Palmer, The Overcomer.

Many times in my life I faced traumatic, painful, gut wrenching circumstances that I just wanted to find an escape from. I cried, became confused and wondered why, what and how. Why me? Why am I going through this? What did I do to deserve this? How am I ever going to get through this?

My earliest memory and introduction to pain was at the hands of my father. I choose this experience because it was one that created a negative conditioning and shaped me at an early age. I want you to know that no matter the trauma, the length of time it has been and how much damage you feel has been done, healing is possible. You can experience your breakthrough, overcome and live a life of peace and freedom.

You see, my father violated and stole my innocence beginning at the tender age of 6 years old. I remember feeling lost, afraid and confused. It was hard for me to understand why he wanted to hurt me and what I did I do to deserve it. The first time he violated me, he forcibly entered me from behind. I was terrified, in extreme pain, broken down and confused. I didn't know what I did to deserve this. I remember the pain from the penetration being so intense that I went numb. My mind and body just wanted to escape but I couldn't move. Little did I know that once the incident was over, the scars would remain.

As my life progressed, I remember feeling broken and needing a lot of help to heal. There was a part of myself/my soul lost, chipped away and as I grew older, I found myself on a path of self-sabotage and destruction. However, while going through the journey, I learned that there was a lot to be gained.

The desire for what I needed as a child became burdensome and muddled. I wanted him, needed him around, cried for him to be there but his presence paralyzed my body with fear. The man that I needed and loved so much, the first man to cherish me and call me his own, was also the same man that bought a silent death to my soul. His actions flooded my consciousness with guilt and shame. He had me on my mother's bed, I didn't belong there with him and he convinced me that I did something wrong. The guilt and shame just poured through me and eventually became a part of me. I was filled with so much fear and pain, that I couldn't control my tears. I couldn't figure out what just happened. He put something enormous in me. I didn't know what it was. All I knew was that it was a punishment for crying and telling him I had a headache after he beat me. He washed me up and told me that WE did something wrong and I couldn't tell my mother. If I did, we would BOTH be in trouble.

My family was all I knew, and I LOVED my mother and brother. I didn't want to be responsible for my family falling apart so I carried that responsibility on my shoulder. I didn't want to hurt my mother and I didn't want to be hurt by my mother, so I kept the secret and hurt myself. I kept my mouth shut so they could stay together but I was slowly falling apart.

I learned to care for another before learning to care for myself. I was stripped of my voice and my innocence; and I became loyal to the perpetrator and internal pain no matter the cost to me. Masking, hiding, muffling my voice, and lying to myself by saying that something destructive wasn't toxic when it was becoming a norm for me. I simply didn't matter.

I lost trust. The man who was to protect me, violated me and taught me that I wasn't worthy of love or protection. The man that was supposed to provide for me eventually left my mother to fend for herself and somehow, I believed it was all my fault. I believed I was horrible for what I did, and I didn't deserve to be a part of my family. It was a very unloving and confusing emotional state that followed me throughout my life. I eventually found myself sabotaging and failing at intimate relationships.

I was a very hurt, broken and confused child that eventually became a very hurt, broken and confused woman. It wasn't until I had my first child, my only daughter that I addressed my hurt and brokenness. I've been on the path of healing ever since. What I've learned is that on this journey of healing is that it's likened to a thorny bed of roses. The thorns will show themselves and they will hurt but getting to experience the rose in all its beauty is well worth it. Thus, the gift that lies in the power to overcome traumatic, life altering experiences is worth the journey.

Yes, my father was an alcoholic and a mental, emotional, physical and sexual abuser. Yes, I was a broken little girl, teenager and woman. And while the pain and mental conditioning seemed to overtake me, there was something greater in me that wanted a different life. The spirit within and the guidance from my Source opened me up to a lifetime of restoration.

What does all of this have to do with you?

You may have experienced unimaginable pain in your past and may have buried it, hidden it, ran from it or allow it to terrorize your heart and mind. If it hasn't come up for healing, then it is more than likely silently terrorizing your life right now. You may not understand why you stay in toxic relationships, sabotage your own success, or not show up for yourself at all. Your unidentified, unaddressed, unhealed past may have something to do with it.

But don't worry… as you have just read, you are not alone. Just as I am healed, so can you be as well. Take a deep breath and now…grab a pen and paper and reflect on where are you are in your life right now. Ask yourself the following and jot down the first thing that comes up: What's ailing you? What's the one thing you don't want to talk about? What pain are you avoiding being present with? What major area of your life are you stuck in? Allow it to surface and release it through the pen. Once you are complete, you may choose to rip the paper to shreds and declare that you are complete. Do it as many times as you need to. It's a powerful healing exercise. The first step is to be aware of what's going on within. It's normal for resistance to heighten when approaching your healing, just be reassured that pain may endure for the night but joy shall come in the morning. Your commitment to the healing journey demonstrates self-love and gives yourself a sense of hope. Just as success leaves clues, so does pain. It leads you to the source of your personal struggles. It allows you to identify where you need to heal and transition from a victim to an overcomer.

An Overcomer is one who prevails, that defeats his/her enemies and a conqueror. It takes work and strength to defeat your enemies whether they are in the form of negative beliefs, traumatic memories, self-sabotage or addictions. It takes commitment and an unwavering belief in yourself and Higher Power to prevail. The healing and personal growth is part of that work and the work isn't always glamorous but what you uncover on the other side is. They are your gifts.

The greatest gift we can receive from overcoming our trials and tribulations is the ability to come in greater alignment with our purpose and our destiny. Through our growing strength and courage, we get to witness the great spirit that dwells within and is constantly evolving and expressing through us.

But how do we get there? There are many paths but ultimately it requires a transformation and renewal of your mind, body and emotions. I invite you to practice as many of the tips provided here to support you on your journey.

Get Clear About What You Want

Earlier on in the chapter, I asked you to write down what was ailing and affecting you negatively. If you did that exercise, you freed up some energetic space and can now allow in what you want to experience.

Can you imagine getting so clear about what you desire to experience that you are able to feel it before it manifests? It may seem easier said than done. During my adversities and struggles I couldn't focus on anything but the problems I was going through. Remember that what you focus on expands, so it is extremely important and beneficial to begin to get clear about what you want. Gaining clarity puts the power back in your hands as you now have a clear vision to bring to life.

The sub-conscious programming that occurred because of incest negatively affected my ability to have healthy, intimate relationships. I constantly felt like my partner was out to hurt me, and I did not trust being in a close relationship with a man. I believed that I was only good for sex and did not know how to commit. I didn't believe I deserved a healthy relationship. When challenged to get clear about what I wanted to experience, I choked. I was so stuck in the pain and didn't have the energy or mental wherewithal to imagine anything different. I felt trapped, and ultimately realized that I needed to decide to get laser-focused on the person I desired to be and the type of relationship I wanted.

Changing this programming took time and it took work. I first began to talk out loud to myself. This was important because it helped my "power thoughts" build strength and resonance within. Soon my power thoughts were louder and stronger than my negative ones and I began to feel happier, more excited, enthusiastic, and grateful for my life. As I built my mental and emotional stamina, I was more receptive to the vision that God had for me. Daily, I began to envision a new me and greater quality relationships. I turned my attention on my vision, practiced clarifying it, even if it were only pieces at a time, and I sharpened the picture in my mind by consistently focusing on it.

With time, I began to add emotion to the vision and it began to take on a life of its own. I share this to demonstrate that even when you feel at your lowest, there is always a glimpse of light for you to gain clarity.

Become What you Want to Experience

Mahatma Gandhi said, *"Be the change* that you wish to see in the world." It was up to me to decide what changes I needed to make. I wanted a loving relationship however, before that can happen, I had to become the love, safety, comfort, and security that I wanted to experience in my relationships. To experience these qualities meant that I had to become the qualities. I began to love myself more deeply by taking time to appreciate everything about me, to speak sweetly to myself, encourage myself more and show myself the care I needed. I began practicing forgiveness regularly, cared for my needs, and released myself from judgment. I am still preparing myself emotionally and mentally for a healthy relationship, but I feel 100% better about myself, having more successful experiences with men and increasingly confident that I will attract an amazing partner in my life.

Raise Your Vibration!

It's important to increase the positive vibrations in your life that will keep you thriving and energetic as you move through adversarial periods of your life. The vibrations of optimism, joy, happiness, love, peace, enthusiasm, and abundance are key to helping you release the sadness, confusion, and pain you may feel when experiencing adversity. To help turn up my positive vibrations, I would greet every morning with an amazing smile and reverence for life. Even when circumstances weren't going right in my life, I found things to be grateful for. I became responsible for how I felt and how I chose to view my life, and I turned up my energy to reflect how amazing and grateful I felt.

I also kept my enthusiasm on high to weaken the depression that could take root at any moment. The higher I turned up my appreciation, gratitude, joy, enthusiasm, happiness, and excitement, the more amazing opportunities began to open for me and the more I was able to contribute by sharing my story. Changes began to occur in my life in ways that I can't explain. I am so excited about the changes in my life and I know that you can see your way out of the current storm of your life as well. I want to share with you some how-to's to help you survive the storm of adversity when you need a "life lift."

1. **Get still**—Learning to meditate will be a tremendous support to you in your life. Find a

practice that works for you. Whether it's a simple relaxation technique or an in-depth, soul-healing meditation practice, get still and go within.

A. For Starters: Guided meditations are great. You can purchase audios or videos to lead you through this process.

B. You can also start meditating in five to ten-minute intervals before you start your day.

C. Get in a quiet space and begin to breathe in through your nose and out through your mouth. Let your thoughts flow. No judgment; don't try to force them to be positive. Be a quiet observer. As you sit and breathe, focus on your breath. Feel it flowing in and out. Imagine yourself breathing in fresh, clean energy and breathing out stress-filled, negative energies. It's important to relax so you can meet these challenging times with grace and ease.

2. **Become the essence of what you desire**—Turn your attention away from what's disturbing and hurtful. This may be difficult at first, but I want you to take the time to practice dwelling on what you want to experience.

A. Identify what you want to experience and breathe life into that vision by imagining how you would feel if you had it.

B. Practice this daily, after or during meditation, while you are shopping, taking a walk, or just enjoying some private time and watch how powerfully you will manifest.

3. **Increase Your Vibration**—Focus on and intensify the good feelings within you.

A. If you find yourself feeling sad or down, talk to yourself positively (either silently or out loud).

B. Speak life into your desires. Speak about the good in your life, the excitement that you will experience when you accomplish your goals, and the good things that will come out of your desires manifesting.

C. Find the smallest things to get happy about. Look at nature and pay attention to all the miracles of life you see there. You are conditioning yourself to find the good.

D. Embrace your current situation and begin to find the lessons in them. This will turn up your confidence and hope, giving you the energy to keep thriving.

4. **Take bold steps forward**—You must do something with all the love, appreciation, strength, and positive energy you've built up.

   A. Create your plan of action. Write down a step-by-step plan of how you want to move forward in your life. This step is easily missed when we are dealing with adverse circumstances because we are so focused on getting out of the pain. When you are creating your plan, be sure to factor in anyone or any circumstance that would be affected by your plans, so you can be successful (i.e. your children's schedules or your budget).

   B. Find a support group, a coach, or professional help to aid you in taking the steps you need to take.

   C. Take baby steps. When moving through and out of adversities, it is often necessary to take small steps at a time.

   D. Keep track of your progress. The victories are so important during this time. Your sense of accomplishment will help you to rebuild your hope and trust in yourself.

E. Move in the face of fear. When you are overwhelmed, remember that the adverse moments will pass, and you have a choice to stay stuck in the same place or to create powerful changes in your life.

Whatever challenge you are facing right now, know that you have the power to overcome. No matter the trauma, length of time you've been suffering or how hopeless it seems; healing is possible. I know that it is scary and sometimes seems like there's no way out, but I want you to keep your faith. Keep the faith that you can break the shackles of mental and emotional bondage and rise above your adversity. With this faith and tenacity, you will experience God's gifts of healing, freedom, peace, abundance, fulfillment and more. I want you to continue to believe in the power that dwells within. You have the power to persevere and push through to overcome!

ABOUT THE AUTHOR

LATALYA PALMER, Founder of Phoenix Rising Success Coaching and Training, mom of 4 amazing children, author and speaker. She is the Creator of "Ignite Your Dreams No Matter What", "Mental Skills Beast Training" programs; and Author of "IGNITE – The Single Mother's Guide to Success, Sensuality and Igniting Your Dreams".

LaTalya's combined experience as a Single Mom, Sports Parent, Cancer Conqueror, training and Certification in Peak Performance and Life Coaching she understands what it takes to mentally raise the bar, break through mental blockages to achieve greater performance levels and greater states of well-being.

It's with the powerful and moving story of her own, that LaTalya can connect with her audience. She shares her bounce back experience after divorce; her transition into single parenthood; going from generational welfare to six-figure income earner; the loss of her mother and her most recent life challenge—the fight against Breast Cancer.

Learn more about this author at www.singlemomsignite.com